I Walked In Santa's Boots

Lowcountry Christmas Memories

Jack Gannon

AUTHOR'S NOTE

All the stories in this book are true.

Names were omitted and, in some cases, locations altered or eliminated to protect individuals' privacy.

Many thanks to everyone who welcomed Santa Claus into your lives; may all your Christmases be bright!

Cover Photo by Captured Moments Photography
509 Adventure St
Beaufort SC 29902
www.cmoments.com

Used with permission

(To read more about the cover photo, please go to page 116!)

For all the children, young and old...

...who still truly BELIEVE!

New cloths

peace on earth

New shoes

Twister

Jumle 2

air hocky

foosball

checkers
board

Letter to Santa from Johnny, 2001

Dear Santa
This is my chrismas list
1. Barbie talking town house
2. treal kitten
3. aquarium
4. Jewlery
5. American Accessories girl
6. furr Real dog
7. books
8. Play horse set
9. horses to the set
10. very own computer
I Love you santa. I have been a good 4 year old girl. You our the best santa claus
Love Eleeleen

Letter to Santa from Eleanor, 2003

A Santa Pic from the Past

I sat beside the colorful decorated Christmas tree in the Old Bay Marketplace, the same as I'd done for many years prior. It was Main Street Beaufort's annual Night On The Town celebration and I, in my guise as Santa Claus, greeted visitors throughout the evening. It was the festival that officially launched Christmas season in Beaufort, South Carolina, as it has the first Friday of every December.

Santa's location for photos was setup midway in the Old Bay Marketplace. The line of waiting children and families formed its own orderly stretch toward Bay Street. It was a pleasant evening, not too hot or too cold, so I was fairly comfortable in my heavy Santa suit, patterned shirt, and white-fur-trimmed black boots. The beard and moustache were securely glued to my face.

Dozens of children patiently waited their turn to visit Santa, not only to take photos with him, but to share stories and Christmas wishes. Many parents had dressed their newborns in tiny Santa suits for their official "First Christmas" photos, and even teens and whole families took photos with him.

At one point there was a break in the line, and Santa was able to take a few peaceful moments to rest. A lady with her teenage daughter approached, and I prepared myself for the next photo session. Instead, the lady asked Santa, "May I show you a photo?"

Santa replied, "Well, of course you may!"

She opened her flip phone and scrolled through her photos folder until she came across a photo of Santa Claus holding a baby. A closer view showed me I was that Santa Claus. "You held my daughter as a baby, and here she is all grown up!" I looked at that photo closer on that small screen, then up at the teenage girl, and smiled, forcing my eyes to crinkle crow's feet. "You've grown into a beautiful young lady," I said to her. To her mother I continued, "Thank you for showing me your wonderful Christmas memory!" I was genuinely touched, in that they both absolutely knew it was the same Santa from so many years in the past.

After a couple more pleasantries they continued on their way into the festive evening. In all my years as Santa Claus, it wasn't often that I was greeted with a returnee from a visit far in the past, so this was quite a treat. They departed, and I sat back, able to return to my short period of rest and remember what it was like way back when I was a child, and one of my own greatest memories of Santa Claus...

A Close Encounter of the Christmas Kind

IT WAS CHRISTMAS EVE!

I was 8 years old, and I lived in Centreville, Virginia. Dulles International Airport was directly to the north across the forests.

I was already interested in meteorology at my young age. My father loved that I was already interested in watching the TV news with him, especially the weather segments. One Christmas Eve we watched WJLA-TV, which covered the Washington, D.C. area.

I grew excited as the weatherman said he would be tracking Santa's flight through the District area of southern Maryland, and then northern Virginia. I asked Dad if I could stay up to watch the 11 p.m. news to follow Santa's flight...but, unfortunately, he said no.

Disappointed, I went to bed, but I worked hard to stay awake so I could get up after everyone else had gone to bed, sneak back to the living room, and turn on the news.

We lived in a two-story house with a mid-level foyer. Mom and Dad's room, and their den, was on the bottom floor. My brothers' and my rooms were on the top, down the hall from the living room where the Christmas tree stood in front of the triple-pane window. The living room curtains were open to face north toward Dulles Airport.

The author's home in Centreville, Virginia, 1969

I snuck out of my room just before 11 p.m. to turn on the TV and wait for the weather segment; The Christmas tree was lit, but there were no presents yet, which meant that I was in time to watch Santa and his reindeer on the weather radar screen. I turned the "On" knob and watched the screen as the large console TV warmed up in time for the 11 p.m. news. I heard the TV screen gently crackle with the static electricity common to the console sets of the 1960s. I paid attention to make sure I didn't fall asleep and miss the weather. At ten past the hour, there was a commercial break followed by the weather.

As he promised, the weatherman quickly went through his forecast so that he could spend more time on the radar scope and the search for Santa in the metropolitan DC skies.

Suddenly I saw it, Santa's icon on the screen. The reindeer and were sleigh flying back and forth across the Maryland area of the scope. He was making great time over Fredrick and Damascus, where Mom's family lived, and over Washington, finally into northern Virginia and over Arlington County first and into Fairfax County—*my county*! The weatherman pointed out that Santa was over Dulles Airport, and the planes were on momentary hold so that he had safe passage through the skies.

I looked out the front window, past the Christmas tree and toward Dulles.

I saw a red light moving in the sky. *It was Rudolph!* I thought to myself. I glanced back at the TV; Santa was over the city of Fairfax and headed for Centreville! I cast another look out the window; that red light was closer!

In a panic, I turned off the TV and quickly ran on my tip-toes to my room. I closed the door and jumped into bed, pulling the covers over my head, just in case Santa looked in to make sure I was asleep.

There was a BUMP from somewhere outside my bedroom door. *Santa's here!* I thought excitedly. *He's on the roof!* I forced myself to sleep, knowing that if I didn't, he'd most likely not leave any presents at our house, and Christmas was going to be ruined because of me...

...and I woke the next morning before anyone else.

There were presents surrounding the tree, all shapes, sizes and colors, glowing from the lights on the Christmas tree! There was even a telescope with my name on its tag. Santa had come, and he hadn't caught me out of bed...I hadn't ruined Christmas for my family...

That one incident, a single *Close Encounter of the Christmas Kind*, would stay in my memory forever. Little did I know what awaited me a quarter century later...

Part 1

The Introductory Claus

"Once Upon A Time..."

Great classic fairy tales and children's stories usually start with "Once Upon a Time". I suppose I can say that the story of my career in an iconic red suit should also start with the same opening.

One day in early 1993 I was reading the daily edition of *The Beaufort Gazette* after it came off the press, just as I did every day at my desk in the Gazette's circulation department. My father, United States Navy Commander John Gannon, instilled in me the discipline to read the newspaper daily when I was in first grade in Hawaii. While I was a cadet at Fork Union Military Academy in Fork Union, Virginia, in the 1970s, he sent me the important news clips and weather maps from the same daily newspaper. Reading a newspaper has always been as natural to me as breathing.

(I was also a semi-regular performer in the Beaufort Little Theatre during my latter high school and early college years. I once worked onstage in college with a ballet company performance of *The Nutcracker Suite* in Charlotte, North Carolina, in a voluntary stagehand position. I especially enjoyed acting on stage after my first role in Neil Simon's *Plaza Suite* while I was a high school senior. The director taught me to portray my role of 'Borden" in such a way that it brought down the house every night. My love of performing and entertaining was born.)

An ad in the Gazette caught my eye.

Main Street Beaufort was taking applications for its downtown Santa Claus. I'd played various characters on stage for the public before, so putting on a red suit and white beard couldn't be that different, right?

I applied for the position. The job required dressing up as Santa, of course, in a suit provided by Main Street. Simply, the job was walking through downtown Beaufort every weekend for minimum wage, riding in the Beaufort Fire Department's antique fire truck for the Christmas Parade, waving to onlookers, appearing downtown for the annual Night On The Town event, and lighting the downtown Christmas Tree accompanied by Mayor David Taub. I submitted an application, and within a couple weeks I'd forgotten about the application, as I'd received no response.

Three months later I received a call. I was hired and was to be Beaufort's new Santa starting with 1993's *Night On The Town*, Tree Lighting, and Christmas Parade for the first weekend of December (the 3rd through the 5th).

Once I was hired, staff members at the Gazette told me they had been interviewed about me, their answers to determine if I was fit to deal with the multitude of children who would be visiting Santa Claus during the Christmas season. I hadn't thought about that; it was, at first, just a part-time job for a little extra cash for my own Christmas. When I learned just how much examination was done, I had a very different view of this new part-time job. If Main Street Beaufort did that much work to decide if I was the right man to play Santa, then I was intent on being the best Santa I could be.

I was told to listen closely when children spoke, whether it was about toys they wanted for Christmas (or even tattletale on their brother or sister...which happened quite often, to my own surprise). More than anything else, it simply needed to be a positive visit they'd never forget. I was given a nice plush suit, a strap-on mustache/beard, and was instructed to be fully dressed and downtown the following Saturday.

Dwayne Buffington/*Gazette*

Santa Claus, with two children in tow, leads a crowd from the Henry C. Chambers Waterfront Park to Bay Street Saturday for the annual tree lighting ceremony.

December 4 1993 Staff Photo by Dwayne Buffington

The jacket was a pullover tunic, with a fake belly and elastic-waist pants that tucked into Santa boot spats. At the time, I didn't think I looked big enough to portray the image of Santa, so I shoved a pillow within the fake belly and drove downtown. I parked in the Piggly Wiggly parking lot on Port Republic Street (*the old store is being restored at this writing; property owner 303 Associates is recreating it into what will be named "Tabby Place"*). I made my way into the rear Marketplace entrance, gathered my wits and prepared to venture onto Bay Street for the first time as Santa Claus.

Of course, I felt a bit tentative, not quite knowing what to expect. It really wasn't much different from performing on stage; before every opening night my stomach was a Kaleidoscope of butterflies! But, I did the job dutifully, walking up and down Bay Street, talking to shopper's downtown, stepping into stores to visit, and posing for numerous photos every weekend. I also sat for studio photos in an empty store in the Marketplace for two Saturdays that December.

I couldn't have anticipated the sheer volume of excitement that awaited me when the photo session staffer opened the door to our makeshift studio. Children were jumping up and down, calling out, "Santa! Santa!" As each child came up for a turn with Santa, the hugs were joyous, warm and loving from every girl and boy. I was truly smiling wide under that beard, although no one could see it. The photos went on, families were happy, and the photos would be ready for pickup two weeks later.

Santa and crew were in one of the empty stores in the Old Bay Marketplace, where the photo set was a simple green backdrop, a bench, balloons, and lots of presents and toy props. One toy in particular was a little Rudolph doll with a flashing red nose. It was popular with many children, and used the most in the photos.

One visit that first year caught Santa off-guard, however. The photo was not to be with a baby or a toddler or child; it was with an elderly couple. They were probably in their 80s, and this photo was for their grandchildren and great-grandchildren. The wife walked with the grace of a Southern Belle, while her husband moved slow and calm like a stoic elderly gentleman. She gently sat down beside Santa, her ankle-length skirt flowing like a cape as she moved. "Hello, Santa," she said, her voice like a musical serenade.

Her husband sat on Santa's other side, picked up the Rudolph doll and held it in his lap. Grumpily he spoke to the photographer. "Tell me when I'm happy."

Santa, glancing at the elderly man, laughed in spite of himself. That was one of the few times Santa didn't give his traditional "Ho-Ho-Ho!"

From the oldest to the youngest: there was also the youngest child ever to get his photo with Santa, and again this was at the beginning of my career in the Red Suit. We (the photographer, staff, and Saint Nick) just wrapped up the final photo shoot of the season in the Old Bay Marketplace when a young lady hurried in, pushing a stroller. She was slightly out of breath, and her long dark hair was unkempt due to her rush from her car to the makeshift studio. She asked if she was in time to get her baby's photo, saying that she had just had her baby only *twelve* hours earlier and wanted to get her to Santa for her First Christmas photo! Well, of course the photographer and Santa couldn't say "no", so they set back up and readied for this beautiful baby's first photo with Santa.

Her mommy was a little sad, as her baby was perfectly happy sleeping in Santa's arms, and wished her tiny one would open her eyes for just enough time to take her photo.

Santa, of course, told her not to worry. He leaned his face toward that snoozing tiny tot and whispered a Christmas secret in her ear. Then he told the photographer to get ready.

Here's how fast it went:

The photographer put her finger on the camera button…

Santa said, "Ready…go!"

Baby opened her little eyes!

Camera clicked and flash flared!

Baby went back to sleep!

Santa spoke very fluent Newborn Baby for that perfect First Santa photo…

Finally, my year as Santa in 1993 ended quietly. With the photos, Night On The Town, Christmas Parade, and sidewalk strolls behind me, I turned in my Santa suit to Main Street Beaufort's manager and collected my pay. Aside from walking around in a bright red and white suit and a couple fun memories, that was it for the season. I had no expectations of being called back for 1994…

The Call Back

Santa Claus anchored Beaufort's annual downtown Christmas parade Sunday afternoon.

© The Beaufort Gazette

December 5 1994 Staff Photo by Bob Sofaly

I never thought about the Santa job again...until late summer 1994, when the manager of Main Street Beaufort called me at work and asked if I'd like to come back as Santa for a second year.

Obviously I'd done something right if the downtown organization was asking me to put on the red suit again. I met with the Main Street manager, picked up my suit, and received my instructions, which was to basically do the same from year before, same pay rate, same events...

However, 1994 would foretell that there was something special, something important, that I could do as Santa. It would no longer be *just a part-time job*…

Goodbye and Hello

It was a typical beautiful day in Beaufort. A sunny mid-60s Saturday afternoon in December 1994 made shopping in the downtown stores a comfortable and enjoyable fare.

Santa slowly walked the sidewalks from west to east along Bay Street and back again. He passed many stores, including the historic Lipsitz Department Store, which sadly closed in 2009.

Santa posed for photos and greeted shoppers and tourists alike, spreading some southern Christmas cheer as best a still-rookie Saint Nick could. The wired mustache and beard was uncomfortable on my face, but after the first year I'd figured how to move my mouth under the prosthetic to make it easier to speak and be heard. I didn't like the way the Santa spats stopped at the tops of the black dress boots. My footwear, to me, didn't look believable. The stage perfectionist in me was disappointed, but I had no alternative to the costume. So the task in my mind was to keep people looking up into my eyes and ignore the footwear cover that would slide down and scrape the sidewalk.

As normal for December, the stores on the southern side of Bay Street cast cool shadows on the west-east sidewalk, so my Bay Street strolls were quicker along the north side in the sun and slower on the south side. I spent more time on the southern sidewalk in order to cool down, as my beautiful jacket and pants did not breathe and actually absorbed the radiating heat of the sun quite well! As well, not shooting photos in direct sunlight did make better photos back in the pre-digital years.

However…

Santa was walking westward on the north side of Bay Street in front of Lipsitz Department Store after having just met a couple children and their mother when a women said, "Santa," from behind. I turned around and saw an elderly lady walking toward me. "Do you have a minute?" she asked.

"Of course," Santa replied.

"I'm sorry," she began.

"I just needed someone to talk to."

"Well, ma'am, I'm glad to be of service, if I can."

"What is your name?"

"Santa Claus."

"Your real name? When you're not all dressed up?"

(This was the first time this question had been asked of me when I was in the Red Suit. My on-stage intuition kicked in and I immediately answered, "Nick.")

She smiled and laughed. "Nick?" she asked back. "Seriously?"

Santa gave a "Ho-Ho-Ho" that was gentle and comforting, not loud and boisterous. *(But, the joke had been made and became a standard answer to similar questions for the next twenty-one years.)*

"Santa…Nick," she continued, "I need help."

This was not going as expected. "How may I help?"

"I lost my husband recently. Our children are all gone with their families, having their own Christmases. So we were going to just have a private Christmas together, and now I'm alone and don't know what I'm going to do."

Instinct kicked in again, and Santa gave her a gentle hug…she began to shake and cry. "It's okay," Saint Nick replied. "You're never alone. Your husband may not be standing beside you, arm in arm, but he is always with you…in your heart. And Jesus loves you, and doesn't want you to despair. You are not alone during this special time of year."

(I really don't know where this came from within me, at that moment, but it felt right. It seemed like this was what she needed to hear.)

"You're right," she finally said as she backed out of the hug. "He is with me in spirit."

"You should call your children. Tell them you'd like to visit them for Christmas."

"I don't drive," she admitted quietly.

"They'll take care of it," Santa said. "Just tell them you don't want to be alone on Christmas. The rest will take care of itself."

(I'd just made a huge mistake…never make a promise or absolute result of any kind while in The Suit.)

She squeezed Santa's gloved hand tightly and gave him a beautiful smile. "Thank you, Nick. I'll do that." She hugged Santa once more and said, "Merry Christmas, Santa Claus."

"Merry Christmas," Santa said, returning the embrace.

She let go and went back the way she came on Bay Street.

(By that time I was roasting in the suit and immediately crossed the street to get back in the shade. That had been a very touching moment for me. I didn't quite know how to process it, but there were children calling to Santa for a visit, and the next hour or so was spent talking with children and families in the cool shade.)

The story was ended, but not concluded…

The next Christmas season, 1995, Santa was again casually walking on Bay Street when the same lady came up to him. This time, however, she was not the sad widow of a year before. She had a happy spring in her step and she gave Santa a big joyous hug. "Thank you!" she said, her voice so alive and animated. "You were so right! I called my children, and told them what you said, and they arranged for me to visit each of them for Christmas and New Year's! And my husband was in my heart the whole time! Thank you, thank you!"

"I'm so glad it all worked out."

"It did, just like you said it would! You really are Santa Claus, Mister Nick!" She hugged Santa again, and then continued on her walk along Bay Street.

("You really are Santa Claus," she said. At that moment something changed in me…I didn't feel like someone dressed in a Santa suit. I felt as though Saint Nicholas, the Patron Saint of Giving, had put me where I was mean to give someone a different present, not one found under a decorated tree in a colorful wrapped box. I had instinctively given someone the gift of hope when it was needed the most…)

I never saw this wonderful lady again, but I can only hope that the rest of her days were happy and fulfilling…

Photos with Santa - Old Bay Marketplace, Beaufort, SC 1994

And the Walls of Jericho...

I learned early in my new Santa career not to break character as Santa Claus. It was easy to do from all the stage shows I'd performed with Beaufort Little Theatre years earlier. Many times over twenty-three seasons that discipline was challenged, but the first time was a biggie.

In my second year as Santa I was again doing studio photos in the Old Bay Marketplace. The set was simple and the same as 1993: green backdrop, bench, presents and dolls as props, and balloons floating from the bench by strings.

The day had gone very well, with many wonderful photos with children. Later in the day, a very happy group of ladies came in for a group photo.

Think about how else to define *very happy.*

How about *eggnog*...without the *eggnog*, that is...at least, the dairy version.

Caught up now? Yes, an absolutely happy group of ladies.

This wasn't the first time I'd dealt with visitors who had participated in some early or extra celebrating during the Christmas season, but this was certainly the largest group I'd dealt with so far in my early days. Well, these wonderful ladies (most were middle-age, just for clarity) were having a great time jockeying for position over who would sit with Santa, sit in the Jolly Old Elf's lap, stood behind, and so on. Stumbling and laughing, they tried to arrange themselves behind the bench, where there really wasn't room, and Santa was focused on the photographer, waiting for the cue to pose for the photo. Suddenly there was a loud crashing sound behind Santa!

The ladies behind the bench had stepped back one step too far, grabbing onto each other to steady themselves, and brought the entire backdrop to the floor! Fortunately, nothing was broken, but it took a little time to put the set back up.

All Santa could say was, "That's the ups and downs of Christmas!"

Grand Marshall Santa

To be perfectly honest, I am very status-quo by nature and like things to be as consistent and unchanging as possible.

When I was told Santa was to be the 1995 Christmas Parade Grand Marshall, my first thought was, "Oh, okay." When I was told Santa would be at the front of the parade, my second thought was, "What?"

Yes, Santa was indeed at the front of the parade, just after the Parris Island Color Guard and Marine Corps Band, instead of in the 1957 Chevy fire truck at the back of the parade. Santa was escorted in a horse-driven carriage filled with Christmas presents on the floorboard at his feet. Runners gave out candy to parade spectators, refilling quickly from the candy boxes on either side of Santa, while the carriage made its way through beautiful Beaufort on that mild December Sunday.

The horse, of course, didn't seem to mind that a big red *Rudolph* dot had been painted on his snout. Sorry, horsey, but there's only one red nose that really glows!

Tribute to "Tootie"

Speaking of the front of the parade, there was a long tradition of a very special Beaufortonian who always led the Christmas parade, and that was a fine gent named Wilson Bourke, more popularly known as *Tootie Fruity*. While he and Santa never met during the parade, his presence at the parade's beginning was just as traditional as Saint Nick bringing up the rear.

Photo courtesy Kathleen and William Harvey

He and his whistle told parade goers that the best parade ever was following him, and he brought the crowds to life with his joie de vivre and genuine Christmas cheer. Rest well, dear sweet man…

Photo courtesy Melanie Gladden

Here Comes Santa Claus!

The first few years of Night On The Town featured evening performances on the stage of the Waterfront Park, which culminated with children leading Santa onstage after the reading of The Christmas Story. The 1995 event was a valuable lesson to me in knowing the Santa legend forward and backward and all necessary stories in between.

The schedule of events was, after various performances, for the city librarian, Dennis Adams, to read the story of Saint Nick. One of our local elementary schools had children performing prior to the reading of the story, and their job was to lead Santa out into the spotlights following the line, "Happy Christmas to all, and to all a good night!"

Santa was to hide in the shadows of the pergola on the Waterfront, but when those delightful children performers peeked into the shadows they all started shouting with excitement, "Santa! Santa! Santa!" Each wanted to hug the Jolly Old Elf's legs, or get picked up, and talk about what they wanted for Christmas.

The experienced stage performer in me wanted it quiet in the shadows so I could listen for the cue to go onstage to the waiting audience, but I couldn't hear anything other than the giggling and excitement of the kids. I was doing the best I could, to no avail, to quiet them down...until...

...one child asked, "Where's Rudolph?"

Inspiration!

Santa replied quietly, "Why, he's flying overhead, leading the reindeer in a circle over Beaufort while I'm here with you!"

The children went to the edge of the shadows to look up into the clear starry night.

The next moment convinced me that God was watching over me that night, as there is no explanation as to what happened next, other than Divine intervention.

A small shooting star quickly crossed the sky.

There was sudden silence in the shadows. The children pointed into the sky, looking for Rudolph's glowing nose, listening for any tell-tale reindeer sounds, and waited for a return arc between the stars.

Time was getting close to go on stage, but the children weren't interested. They had seen Rudolph's glowing nose cross the sky and wanted to see it again. Santa finally prodded, "You've all done such a wonderful job tonight that Rudolph slowed down enough for you to get a peek of him guiding my sleigh! But we have to finish the show, so why don't you all pretend to be my reindeer and lead the way?"

The rest of the night went perfect. The children were great, singing "Here Comes Santa Claus" with incredible excitement and joy. They led Santa and the gathered audience to the nearly 15' city Christmas tree across from the Best Western. We all gathered for the traditional tree lighting with Mayor Taub. The tree was adorned with hundreds of beautiful, colorful lights...the perfect spot to take Christmas photos, with the Beaufort River in the background.

The tree eventually had to be replaced, and today stands a good 30'…an extraordinary site when lit at night.

Whenever I've seen a shooting star since then, I've always said "Thank you" for that miraculous Christmastime present when I needed it the most.

Santa waving to the crowd at the Waterfront Park, 1995

It's a Bird, It's a Plane, It's Super-Girl!

Another fun story from a photo shoot inside the Old Bay Marketplace in downtown Beaufort: the set was in place and Santa assumed his position on the bench. The presents were colorful, stacked and well-balanced on both sides, balloons floated in the background, and the Rudolph doll was prominently in place, without a blinking nose, however.

The window in the empty store was blocked to keep anyone from looking in while Santa got settled in place, and the door closed. The photographer, Sue Jarrett, peeked out the door to get a look at the line of people. She closed the door quickly and with a smile, she said, "The first girl in line is *so* excited! She's jumping up and down, she can't wait to see you!"

Santa steadied himself and said, "Let's do it!"

An assistant opened the door, and as he prepared for a happy child, he didn't notice that the photographer was already posed to take a photo. That happy little girl bolted into the room and, with her momentum at full speed, leapt into the air to land on Santa with a big hug. The photographer caught that perfectly-timed moment of the girl in this photo just as she landed!

Photo © The Beaufort Gazette

December 14 1997 Staff Photo by Sue Jarrett

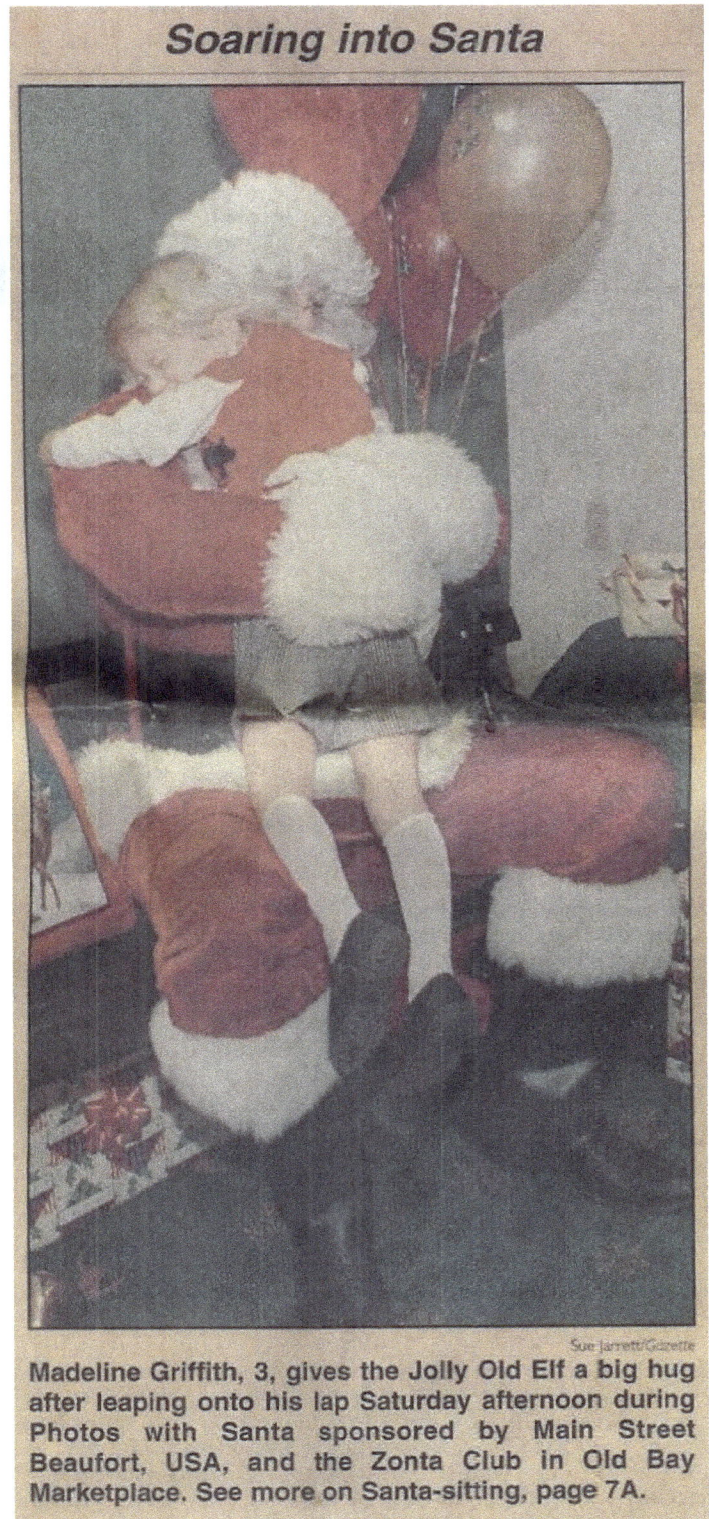

Soaring into Santa

Sue Jarrett/Gazette

Madeline Griffith, 3, gives the Jolly Old Elf a big hug after leaping onto his lap Saturday afternoon during Photos with Santa sponsored by Main Street Beaufort, USA, and the Zonta Club in Old Bay Marketplace. See more on Santa-sitting, page 7A.

Part 2

The Family Claus

The First Elf

Night On The Town 1994 was my second year as Santa, and the ninth year of Night On The Town by Main Street Beaufort. Santa's job was to walk around the downtown streets, which were closed off to traffic the first Friday of December. I learned in my first year that the crowds were simply too large for Santa to travel far by foot. So the second year I stayed fairly close to the intersection of Bay and Charles, close to where I would need to be for the reading of the Christmas story after 8 pm.

Essentially Santa stood in one spot, slowly rotating so as to interact with the crowd which had completely surrounded him. Saint Nick was talking with two little boys, probably three or four years old, when two teenage boys did the unthinkable and inexcusable...

They ran up behind Santa and pulled down his beard, revealing my *real* face to those little boys. Wide-eyed, their little faces twisted into shock and disbelief.

All I could do was hold the beard up to my face, its elastic straps stretched out from beneath the tight-fitting wig, until I could go inside Lipsitz Department Store and ask to use their restroom to cinch the facial hair back into place. I was more upset that those little boys' memory of Santa was ruined than I was angry at the smart-alack teenagers. By now I hope those two teens have grown up with children of their own who did not experience the same kind of shock they caused, and hopefully feel some regret as to the result of their actions so long ago.

But it also taught me a lesson: I needed a bodyguard. I also needed better Santa facial hair.

Santa and elf Julie, 1995

Private life changes had me living with my parents for much of the following year, and it was there that I met their apartment building landlord couple. Their daughter worked at a restaurant over on Lady's Island, and had a niece living there at the time. Conversations over the months revealed to them that I had played the part of Santa for the last two years. That young niece, perhaps twelve or thirteen years old, asked if she could help Santa. It was a great idea! Dressed as an elf, she could be the bodyguard Santa needed to watch his back. Night On The Town 1995 introduced Santa's elf Julie, with the story that she had earned the special "elf credits" at the North Pole Workshop to accompany Santa to Beaufort.

During that season she rode on the Beaufort Fire Department's antique firetruck with Santa in the Christmas Parade, and stayed by his side during Night On The Town and at the Tree Lighting. She also strolled with him during the weekends of December to greet the tourists and downtown Christmas shoppers. Over the next twenty years, two other young ladies would work as elves / bodyguards...plus another special addition to the Santa Family which created a major influence in nearby towns...

Jolly good time

Sue Jarrett/Gazette

Callie Burdiss, 3, tells Santa Claus what she wants for Christmas as her mother Savannah listens Saturday afternoon at Old Bay Marketplace. The Jolly Old Elf will be back listening to wishes and posing for photos next Saturday from 1 to 4 pm courtesy of Mainstreet Beaufort.

© The Beaufort Gazette

December 8 1996 Staff Photo by Sue Jarrett

The Second Elf

Something was pointed out to me years later. From a distance, children often think Santa Claus is probably the coolest guy around! But up close Santa many times can seem quite scary. Some children suddenly realize that Santa *knew* if a child had been good or bad that year...and they didn't want to take the chance of being caught! This was where The Elf came into play. Santa's Elf had two jobs: keep an eye out for any potential threat to Santa's person from all directions, and to receive the children who were too rattled to visit Santa personally. What made it work even better was those children got to speak to someone from The North Pole with the assurance that Santa would get their Christmas wishes. In 1995, my third year in The Red Suit, was the first year with an elf helper, and the Main Street events went a little smoother. It also drew a lot of attention from the crowd, seeing a young elf riding in the antique fire truck with Santa.

Julie could not continue as The Elf in 1996. She was excellent in her job working with children who were too skittish to sit on Santa's lap, but after only one year she couldn't return for a second. So, her cousin Kelly took on the mantle of The Elf.

The Elf was a calming influence to scared children, and eventually became a popular photo moment for children who wanted a photo with The Elf in addition to, or instead of, Saint Nick.

Santa Claus with Elf Kelly and the author's
wife Mendy, 1996

Mrs. Claus

The Santa Family added its final, but pivotal, member in 1997...just little over a year after I got married.

When we were dating, Mendy came to the Marketplace to get her first photo with me as Santa Claus. She needed to know what she was getting into when she married me, which was basically me gone most December weekends as I walked Beaufort's downtown streets in a hot Santa suit.

An idea formed in my head and I asked her a question. After spending our first December weekends apart while dating, why not join me as "Mrs. Clause"?. It took a little persuading but she finally said "yes".

As this was still in the early days of the Internet, I had no idea where to find a "Mrs. Claus" costume, so the old stage performer in me took over and I improvised by purchasing another Santa suit, and she wore a black skirt or Christmas-style skirt and boots with the Santa jacket, spare wig, and Santa hat.

Like me, Mendy was a stage performer...in fact, that was where we met, and we performed a few shows together for the Beaufort Little Theatre before she joined me for the biggest audience we would ever have: The City of Beaufort for Night On The Town and the Christmas Parade.

Santa Claus, now with Mrs. Claus and Elf Kelly in tow, descended on the evening event to thousands of waiting celebrators...and they were collectively a massive hit! Already being married made Santa and Mama Claus' relationship totally genuine to the public that night and a new dynamic began. Not only did children want their photo with Santa, they also wanted photos with Mrs. Claus, both with Santa and with her alone, and they wanted photo with Elf Kelly, too, and then entire families wanted photos with the whole Santa Family. Even in the pre-digital camera age we began taking many more photos with families as the lines began to increase.

Mrs. Claus, Santa, and Elf Kelly, 1997

In the Sunday Christmas parade, we all rode on the back of that antique fire truck, and not only were the gathered crowds calling for Santa, they also called for Mrs. Claus!

The Santa Family with Mayor and Mrs. David Taub

© The Beaufort Gazette

December 8 1997 Staff Photo by Sue Jarrett

Boombears

After four years the Santa photo opportunity moved from the Marketplace to BOOMBEARS, an upscale toy store just a few blocks to the east on Carteret Street.

The Christmas photo set was in the fenced outside courtyard facing Carteret (while the business is long-gone, the building is still there). Santa was seated in front of a cross-hatched wall the first year, unable to see the line of children waiting behind him. Aside from the novelty of appearing as Santa at a toy store, there is one incredible memory that stands out from the couple of years we did Santa photos there...

As I said, the line was at an angle and I wasn't able to see who was next in line. I will note that this was a great teaching time for me to learn how to judge the children's personalities within seconds. I was surprised when a mother placed her young daughter in my arms as I heard a distinctive plastic *clunk* when the girl was settled on my lap. "She can't walk, Santa," the mother said softly. "She just got fitted with her new legs."

That's when Santa peered down slightly, in an attempt to make sure the little girl didn't think he was staring. Two tan-colored artificial legs extended from beneath a beautiful red Christmas dress. As the son of a Navy medic, I'd seen plenty of people over the years with artificial limbs, so I was less surprised than I was sympathetic...but even that emotion was set aside.

This little girl gave not one thought about her man-made legs. She happily talked about her school grades and hobbies and helping around the house, never once talking about how she was limited in doing anything! At one point she even said, "Don't my new legs look great, Santa?"

Emotion stabbed at my heart, and had I let myself I would have cried. I was incredibly honored to be with such a strong little lady!

"They are absolutely beautiful," Santa replied, trying hard not to choke from that lump in his throat.

It was what she said next, that remains to this day, one of the most memorable moments of my Santa career.

"What would YOU like for Christmas, Santa?"

I was stunned! I had no words, but I forced myself to answer with something. I could only say the first thing that came to mind.

"You are a wonderful young lady to ask such a touching question," Santa replied cheerfully. "But what would I like for Christmas? Well...I'd like you to work real hard and practice using your beautiful new legs and walk up to me next year and tell me about your year. That would be the best Christmas present I could ever receive."

We talked another minute or so, and then the mother lifted her daughter from my arms and wished Santa a Merry Christmas.

The next year Santa was in the same location with the same basic setup, but I was better positioned to see who was in line...and I saw that same girl. She had grown a bit, of course. She was actually standing in line with her mother. When it was finally her turn to visit ole' Saint Nick, she didn't walk, no, not at all...

She RAN...

Over the decades I was asked again what Santa wanted for Christmas...but that little girl's gift of running to see Santa was simply the best.

Unfortunately, after Boombears there would not be another formal photo opportunity in Beaufort for Santa visitors for many years...

Mendy, Santa Claus, Elf Kelly at Boombears 1998, the last Santa portrait event in Beaufort in the 20th Century

A Special Present Request

With the advent of the Santa Family in Beaufort at Christmastime also came the tricks of the trade to preserve *The Reality of the Illusion*, our official Santa Motto. Parents would start passing early word via Elf Kelly or Mrs. Claus to softly tell Santa things like the child's name in advance, or how he/she is doing in school, special awards or such secrets only Santa could know outside the family. We crafted a perfect line of communication totally secret from many of the children!

Special requests also began. One early one was from Beth, my coworker at The Beaufort Gazette. I'd seen her daughter Sami many times in the office. Beth, of course, knew I was Santa from the days in December I either had to leave early or not work on a weekend. One day she asked for a favor...

Sami, a young girl of six or seven, asked her mom Beth to ask Santa to leave a special present so that she would know, for sure, that Santa had stopped by their house on Christmas Eve. She asked for Santa to bring Frosty the Snowman along on his journey and to leave a little piece of snow behind when they were in her house.

By this time, I'd established my first Santa Claus email address and business card. I gave Beth one of my cards and, after Sami was asleep, Beth left one of my cards and a little spilled puddle of water on the floor.

The next morning, I was told, Sami was beyond excited with what she found on her bedroom floor! Though the snow had apparently melted her special request had been answered!

In following years, she asked for one of Santa's gloves and a bell from Rudolph's harness... And every year when Sami visited Santa downtown she knew that he was the real Santa because he asked how she like her special presents...

"That's Not the Real Santa"

With the Santa Family established and working smoothly, Beaufort visitors got used to seeing Santa with Mama very quickly. We made such an impact so rapidly, that one day I saw in our newspaper that a nearby town had added a Mrs. Claus to its parade! Mrs. Claus began showing up in other regional Christmas Parades...that was a proud tradition to have started!

Another co-worker brought her daughter to wherever we appeared downtown, and, like Sami, I naturally knew special details because her mother shared them when we were at work in preparation for their visit to Santa. This co-worker one day passed on something that her daughter said.

They had just visited Santa and Mama in downtown Beaufort, where Santa told them that The Merry Couple was departing to return to the North Pole. They went to a store the next day where the store had an employee dressed in a store-quality suit (*I'll discuss the nature of suits soon*). She asked her daughter if she'd like to visit with this Santa. Her daughter said, "That's not the real Santa."

Her mother was surprised but asked her, "How do you know that?"

"Because," the little girl replied, "the real Santa travels with his wife!"

43

The First Improvement

Now that I knew I was in for the long haul, I looked at Santa and Mama's physical appearances. We were fully using computers then and could start shopping online for specialty items, where I found an actual "Mrs. Claus" dress and bonnet and a higher-quality suit for myself. I settled on a traditional Santa suit that was a zip-up jacket rather than pullover tunic, but still wore the original spats that came with the first suit. Our new suits arrived before the next Christmas season.

Another change was the facial hair. Still remembering that night those two teens pulled down my beard on Bay Street, I decided I needed to find something I could glue on instead.

It took some searching, as I was learning how to navigate the Internet. I finally found a supplier who sold high-quality wigs, beards, and glue-on mustaches. I ordered my first set and tried it on when I received it.

It was so much better! My mouth was actually visible, and when I spoke my jawline and beard moved without the mustache dropping down. Even though artificial, the beard finally moved like a natural one. I even took the additional dramatic step of perfecting my Santa voice since I could actually be heard well with the new facial hair construction. I studied the Santa voices from *Santa Claus* (1985, with David Huddleston as Santa), *Rudolph The Red Nosed Reindeer* (1964, with Stan Francis voicing Santa), and *Miracle On 34th Street* (1947, with Edmund Gwenn as Kris Kringle), among others. I settled on the particular inflections of these three for my speaking voice, my loud voice (to be heard over the crowds as needed), and my joyous voice for children and families. I also took the extra precaution of gluing down the beard even though I thought it probably wasn't really needed. It turned out that was another moment of Divine inspiration, however; during Night On The Town in my new suit and hair, I had a little boy with dark curly hair climb onto my knee and without missing a beat said, "You're not the real Santa."

With my Santa voice fairly perfected, as I'd practiced dropping my natural baritone down to a gentle bass while in The Red Suit. "Why do you say that?" I asked much like Edmund Gwenn.

He patted my chest. "That's a pillow."

Well, he was wrong on that count, it was not a pillow but it was an extra layer of padding. Without lying I replied, "Actually what you just thumped is a few layers of clothing. It's very cold at the North Pole, and flying reindeer at jet altitudes is a bit cool up there."

He thought about that for a moment, and then protested again, "That's not a real beard."

It was time for the *test under fire*, I thought. So, again channeling Ed Gwynne in "Miracle On 34th Street", Santa said, "Go ahead, give it a tug." *But I had discreetly slipped my hand underneath the beard to hold it in place...just in case.*

That little boy, probably seven years old, reached a hand up and gently grabbed the side of the beard, where the amount of glue used to secure the beard was thickest by all perfect chance. He began to pull down, and reflexively I started lowering my face, but he was still faster and I expected my face to be revealed a second time.

Not this time, however. My cheek flesh began to stretch from the pull of the glued-on beard by that small hand. He let go, and my head jerked back up in response. His little eyes were wide open in shock. "Santa! Santa, I'm so sorry! I believe, I really do! You're real! I'm sorry! Can I ask for just one present?"

The Reality of the Illusion was not only maintained, but secured...pun absolutely intended!

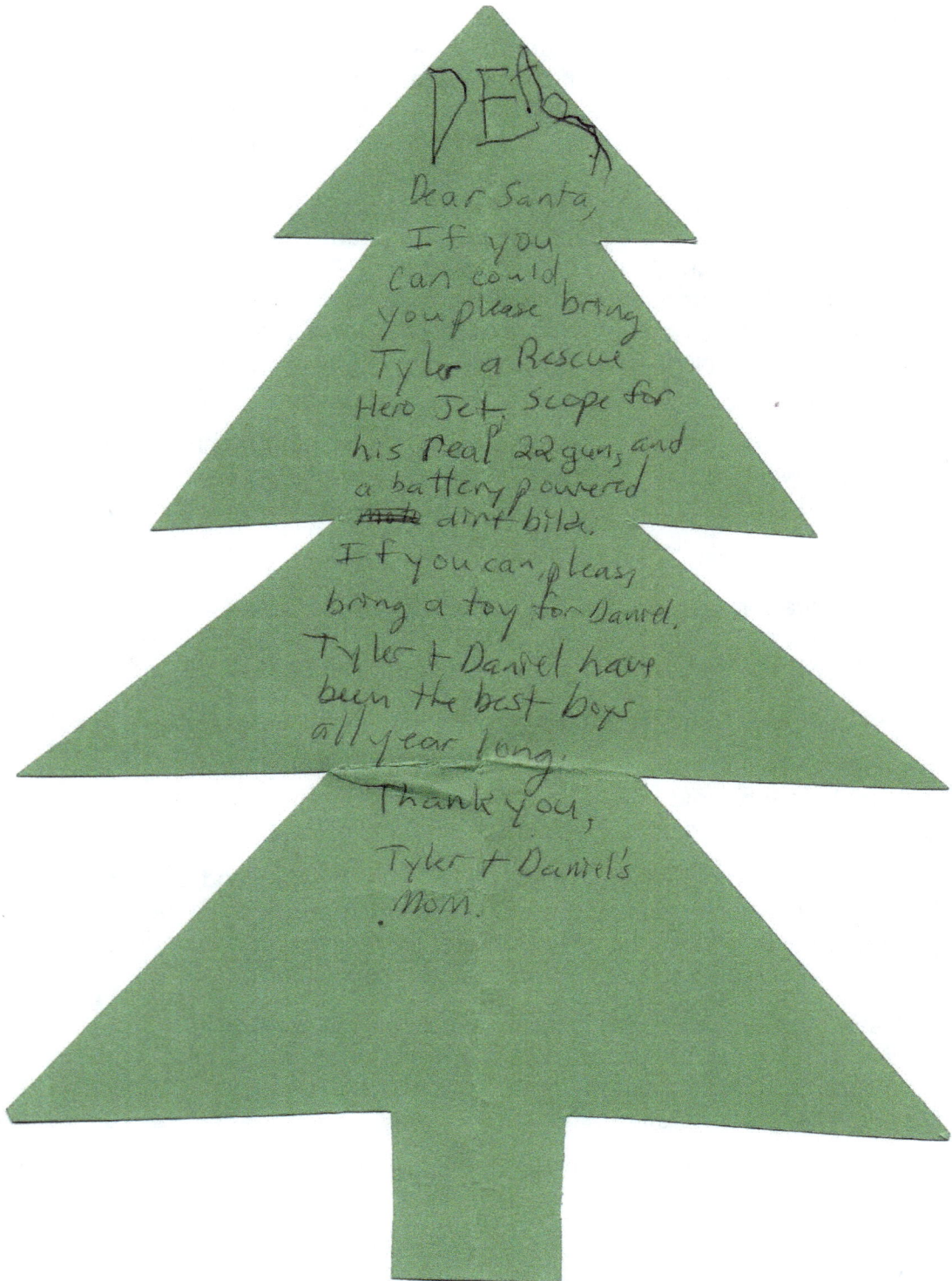

Dear Santa,

If you can could you please bring Tyler a Rescue Hero Jet, scope for his real 22 gun, and a battery powered dirt bike.

If you can, please bring a toy for Daniel.

Tyler + Daniel have been the best boys all year long.

Thank you,

Tyler + Daniel's Mom.

Tyler and Daniel made sure Santa saw their 2003 wish list!

My Wish List

Dear Santa:

Batman

Penguin

_____

_____

_____

Your Friend,

Michael

Sometimes letters are long, sometimes they're short. Michael's letter in 2004 was very precise!

Part 3

The Expansion Claus

The Call That Changed It All

We were ready for Night On The Town and Christmas Parade 1997. However, before Main Street Christmas weekend arrived I received a phone call. The lady on the other end identified herself as working for Fripp Island Recreation, and she had gotten my contact information from Main Street Beaufort. They were in need of a Santa.

For many years they'd had their own Santa performer for Thanksgiving weekend. That event was a fire truck Friday evening entrance at sundown to the waiting guests at the Beach Club to lead the crowd in lighting the buildings' Christmas lights, and on Saturday morning to visit with diners in the Beach Club for Breakfast with Santa. Their Santa could only appear Friday night, and they needed a fill-in for Saturday morning. I agreed to take on the job, and asked if my wife could come along as Mrs. Claus, which was happily accepted.

We arrived at the Beach Club on the Saturday morning after Thanksgiving and outfitted ourselves in a service hallway. When we stepped downstairs into the dining area, we were met by many excited children waiting to see Santa. They were all quite surprised to see Mrs. Claus in tow! We learned a couple things which were extremely important after that weekend, however:

Fripp Island Elf "JT" with Santa and Mama Claus at *Breakfast With The Clauses*

First, Mrs. Claus was a hit with the Fripp Island children. Those who were too skittish to visit with Santa were more than comfortable visiting with Mrs. Claus to ask for Christmas presents. Second, and unfortunately more important, was that the children left confused...because the Santa they saw at breakfast was absolutely not the same Santa they saw the evening before. The suits were different, the hair was different, even the characters and demeanor were different. But, we did our job and returned home to do the regular Main Street Christmas weekend and other duties.

Fast-forward to summer 1998...I received a follow-up call from Fripp Island Recreation. They wanted to hire us both for Friday night as well as Saturday morning! Apparently there were a lot of calls where families' children noticed that there were two different Santas and didn't understand why. We were, however, invited back for the entire Thanksgiving weekend this time! Thus began the annual tradition of Santa and Mrs. Claus beginning the Christmas season by arriving on Fripp Island on Thanksgiving Friday evening and returning on Saturday morning for *Breakfast with The Clauses* for the next eighteen years.

We ended up buying Mrs. Claus a second costume, as her first one, like my suits, was heavy. It didn't breathe well but retained heat exceptionally well! We bought her a lighter-fabric dress with apron and bonnet, which she wore for her Fripp Breakfast events. The first time she wore it on Fripp Island during the Saturday morning event, children started thanking her for making their breakfasts! It hadn't dawned on us that her outfit looked just like she'd come out of the kitchen!

Speaking of the kitchen, there is one special little girl who will always remain deep in Santa's heart for her own Christmas dedication and tenacity. Over the years the crowds at Fripp Island grew annually for the grand Beach Club lighting and first visit with Santa in upper Beaufort County. One particular such Thanksgiving Friday evening the local weather had gotten quite chilly, although Santa and Mama Claus, being from the North Pole, were quite comfortable despite the nearly three-hour-long line. Finally, though, Santa and Mama could see the end of the line beyond the brilliant flood lights which allowed for many excellent nighttime photos. The last child to take a photo was a lovely young blond-haired girl in a bright blue down jacket, holding a glass of milk and a plate with three chocolate chip cookies! "These are for you, Santa," she said happily and proudly, despite a slight shiver in her voice from the chilly air.

"She held them all night," her mother told the Clauses. "I said I could hold them for her, but she insisted on giving them to you herself."

Santa smiled and welcomed that charming, dedicated little lady to sit with him for her special Christmas photo…milk and cookies included!

The First Christmas Show...and Cover Photo

The year 1999 brought the opportunity to combine my love of the stage and Santa Claus. Beaufort Little Theatre put on a special Christmas show: "Sounds of the Season". Mendy and I appeared in this comedy musical show with other regular Beaufort Little Theatre performers, with whom we had appeared in other shows, in a Christmas-themed variety show on the stage in the Beaufort Naval Hospital auditorium.

I brought two Santas to the show: the first Santa was in a comedy skit at the end called "Keep The Home Fires Burning", which featured Mendy's and my own years-long dentist Gary Ayers as the stereotypical "dastardly villain" trying to destroy Christmas for a poor old woman. Santa Claus appeared to challenge the villain, Whipley Skidmore, to a contest when he tried to foreclose on the mortgage on Mother Kindlady's (Mendy) home. Santa turned the moment into a game show and beat Whipley when he asked the villain "What is your name?" When the time ran out, stagehands ran out and started wrapping Reynolds Wrap around Whipley as he groaned, "Foiled again!"

After the show Santa barely had time to change from the stage version to the high-quality Beaufort suit to meet the children in the lobby. Finally, after the audience left, Sue Jarrett hung back with Santa to take photos of him in front of the stage Christmas tree. That image ended up as the cover of the November 29, 1999 Beaufort Gazette Holiday Gift Guide.

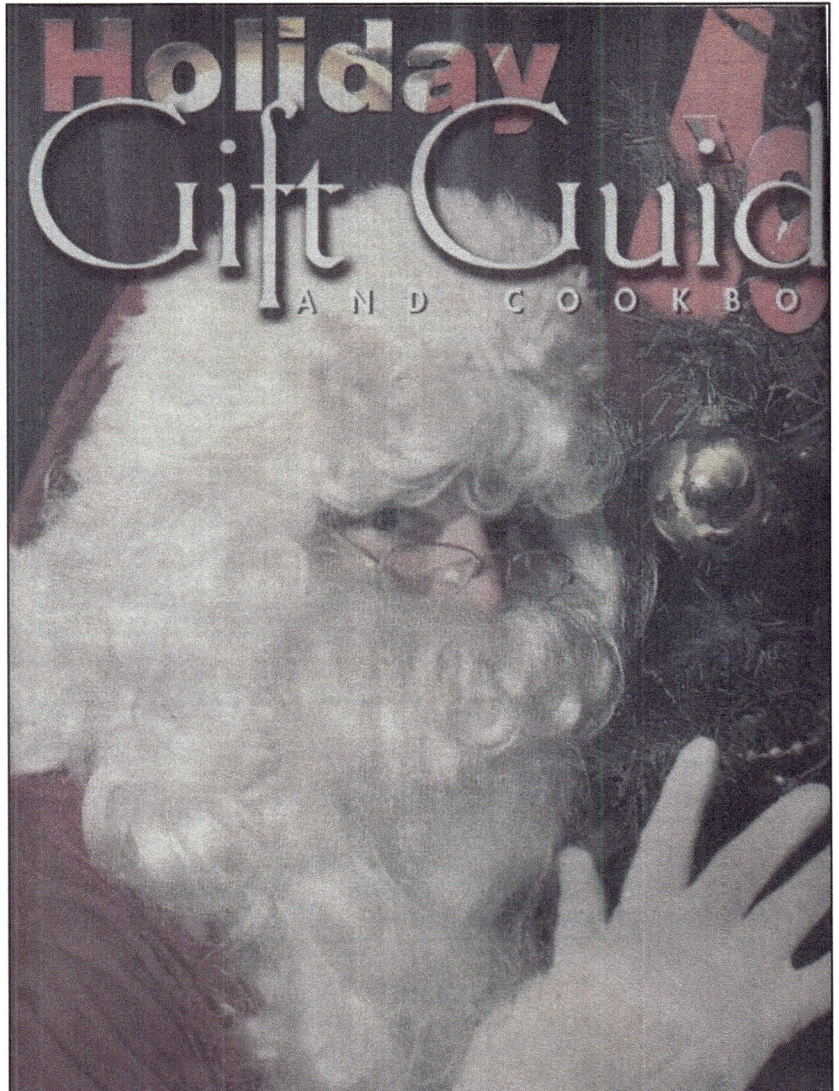

Photo © The Beaufort Gazette

November 29 1999 Staff Photo by Sue Jarrett

A New Look or Two...or Three...

Even the better Santa suits wear out from extended use. Now that I'd doubled our joint appearances between Beaufort and Fripp Island, it was time to replace my second Santa suit. I found a beautiful old-world style hooded brocade with burnished gold trim on the sleeves and jacket hem just above the white fur. It was the same style as was on the good Mrs. Claus dress, although her trim was red-accented rather than black. The brocade came with a brown belt and brown spats, however. That wouldn't do, not at all! Additionally, the original black spats were dead and unusable, so ingenuity took over. I bought a pair of black rubber boots and white-fur strips at Walmart, along with plenty of Superglue, to make my own pair of Santa boots!

The first time Santa and Mama appeared in their *formal* outfits, they looked spectacular! I cannot remember how many comments we received about how great they looked. Over time I added a second *formal* suit, another Mrs. Claus dress midway between the formal dress and the breakfast one, plus a new Santa suit which included a candy-cane shirt and overalls with gold buttons down the front, and the jacket itself, while traditional, was longer and had pockets! The multiple costume versions became synonymous with Beaufort's Santa Claus...

Studio Photos courtesy Captured Moments Photography, Beaufort SC

www.cmoments.com

Another Island Event

Fripp Island Recreation called annually to make sure we were returning to ring in the Christmas season, and then also asked if we were available to appear on nearby Cat Island at the then-South Carolina National Golf Club. They even brought over the fancy "Santa throne" for me to sit in. Who was I to say "no"?

One special appearance on Cat Island wasn't the actual visits with children, but Santa's unusual arrival. A local car dealership owner lent his private helicopter for St. Nick to get a chopper escort from the Beaufort airport to the golf green behind the Cat Island clubhouse! Santa truly was flying across Beaufort's beautiful landscape, with nothing between his boots and the marshes below but the cockpit glass bubble. The chopper landed gently on the green to many cheering families and excited children! This was Santa's version of a Ho-Ho-Hole in one!

Santa and Mrs. Claus arriving on Cat Island in style: in a red golf cart!

The Santa Family Motto and Saint Nicholas

The Reality of Illusion was the motto of the Santa Family at every appearance, because of that incident on Bay Street by those teens in front of those small children. As long as I was to wear The Red Suit, I was going to be Santa completely, and that meant knowing the true history of Saint Nick.

Santa Claus of the present is derived from the real Saint Nicholas, born March 15, 270, and lived until December 6, 343, in the Roman Empire. He was not only the Patron Saint of Giving, but also the Patron Saint of children, sailors, fishermen, merchants, and more (Wikipedia). He was the son of wealthy parents in Turkey, who died while Nicholas was young, and the orphan was raised by his uncle Nicholas, the Bishop of Patara. Nicholas the elder eventually ordained the younger as a priest. In 317 he was consecrated Bishop in Myra.

While Nicholas is attributed with miracles that led to his sainthood, one event in particular is what helped lead toward the legend of "Saint Nick" today: a poor man had three daughters but could not provide proper dowries for them, meaning the girls would remain unmarried and become known as harlots, whether in reality or in rumor. Nicholas heard of the girls' plight, and under cover of night threw three purses filled with gold coins through the window opening of the house, one for each daughter. (Wikipedia)

Another legend, which had a deep personal connection to me, was that Nicholas would do secret gift-giving by putting coins in the shoes of those who left them outside for him, which today is celebrated on his feast day December 6 in western Christianity and December 19 in eastern Christianity. I attended first grade at Saint Anthony Catholic School in Honolulu, Hawaii. On Saint Nicholas' feast day our teacher, Sister Ann, told all us first-graders to put one shoe each outside the back door of the classroom and return to our desks with our heads down. (Take a little time to laugh at the image of a class full of Catholic students putting a shoe in a row outside the door and hopping back on their shod feet to their desks!) The marvel was that only moments later we heard bells jingle outside the door, and a bellowing "Ho Ho Ho!", and Sister Ann let us scurry out the back door...actually, it was more like chaos because no one hopped this time but ran on both feet out the back door. All the shoes along the back wall had candies in them! Everyone retrieved their shoes and I stood alone beside mine. Looking back and forth along the length of the building toward the tree line, I watched while multiple classes of students retrieved their shoes. I wondered how Saint Nicholas could have filled all those shoes in mere moments, and that Christmas mystery has stuck with me through the decades.

This childhood memory eventually worked itself into my own Santa persona, with the help of Santa's elves. One of the elves would deftly slip a small plastic-wrapped candy cane into Santa's hand so Santa could make a Christmas treat magically appear out of thin air for each visiting child!

Returning to the earlier subject of the other Santa in the retail store, I would often deal with the question of how I got from one place to another in a different suit, in a few minutes, due to other fine gents appearing as Saint Nick. While I was now the official Santa for Beaufort, Fripp Island, and Cat Island, I knew that stores had their own Santa Claus, rural fire departments had their own, and even once a competing visiting Santa and Mrs. Claus appeared at Night On The Town. The easiest answer was also the most believable, when attributed to the legend of Santa Claus: the same magic that allows Santa to traverse the globe in one night on Christmas Eve allows him to move several blocks while children and families walked or drove. As for Santa's change of attire, Saint Nick always wore the appropriate suit for each venue, which is why he wore the standard jacket in the stores, but for special events he wore the long coat or brocade. This answer worked every time, because I never said the other Santas were *Santa's helpers*, but we were all actually one and the same.

𝔑ot 𝕿oying 𝔄round

Barbie, Ken, Frisbee, Cabbage Patch Dolls, and so on...they are the typical toys amongst so many which children asked for each year. It had always been easy for Santa to have conversations about toys.

Until one child sprung a surprise on me.

On one last 1990s Breakfast with The Clauses on Fripp Island a child asked for a Giga Pet.

I remember asking myself, *"What the heck is a 'Giga Pet'?"*

The only thing Santa could say was, "Which one?"

The little boy proceeded to tell me all about this mysterious toy. His descriptions helped me with the other dozen or so requests for the same toy that morning. That lesson: when in doubt, get the child to tell you about the toy you're already supposed to know all about.

After that weekend I hurried to Kmart and Walmart and walked the toy aisles until I found the *Giga Pet*, plus a bunch of others I'd never seen before. It was a good task, as during the rest of the season more children asked for that toy specifically plus many of the others I'd just discovered on the toy shelves.

Every November, as soon as Halloween items were taken down in the stores, I'd walk all the local toy aisles and study the new toys and new versions of old toys. Never again was Santa caught off guard!

A Miracle on Bay Street

With the Santa Family complete, it was much safer for Santa to walk among the visitors and revelers during Night On The Town. Mama and one or two elves not only watched the people behind Santa as he chatted with children but guided him around to meet with all the families which had encircled him.

Santa definitely got a workout on Bay Street: lifting children, and posing with babies and all their family members together for crowd photos.

During one Night On The Town in particular, the Santa Family was again encircled by the chattering crowd, when Mrs. Claus quickly pulled Santa to his left, away from the direction he was turning. "Santa," she said loud enough for the gathered crowd to hear easily, "you have

a very special visitor tonight. This family is from France, and this is their first visit to Beaufort and Night On The Town. Their youngest daughter doesn't speak English and doesn't really understand what's going on. Her parents told her that you didn't speak French, but I told them you had a surprise for her."

Santa looked down at the beautiful blonde lass, her blue eyes sparkling with the excitement of the night but also showing confusion. He happily nodded in greeting at her parents, and smiled wide enough that his eyes crinkled as he knelt down before that uncertain child and said…

"Bonn soirée! Mon nom est Papa Noel, mais ici je'm appelé Santa Claus. Comment allez-vous ce soir?"

The crowd fell silent as it observed Santa Claus speaking to that little girl in her own language.

"Vous pouvez parler à moi! Vous êtes vraiment Papa Noel!"

Her parents' eyes were wide and tearing in joy and surprise, as were many of the closest bystanders.

For the next couple of minutes the proverbial pin drop could have been heard on the street as all watched Santa give the greatest Christmas present ever…the entire world…to one special little girl. He was *her* Santa!

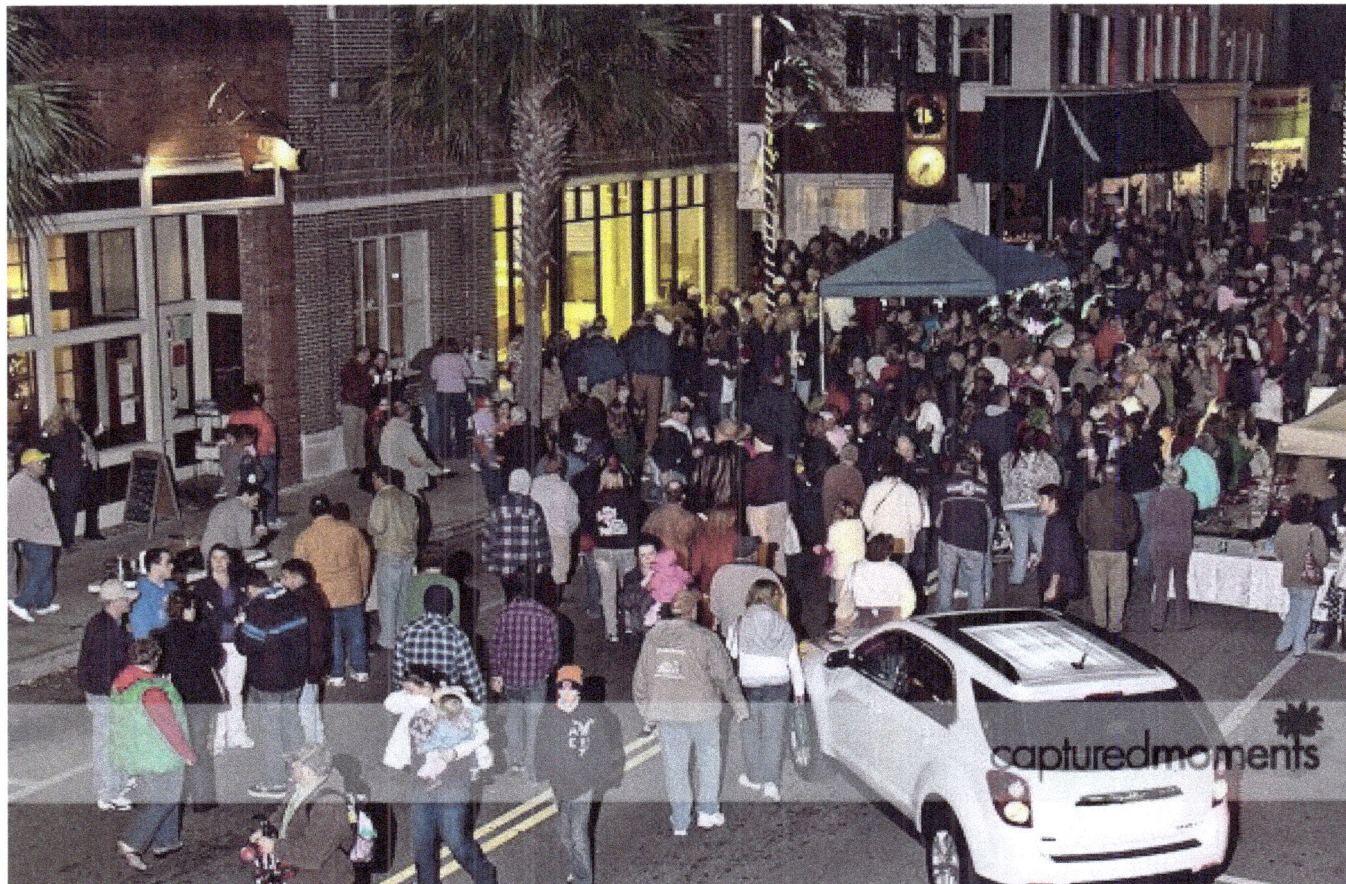

Photo Courtesy Captured Moments Photography

www.cmoments.com

For Those in Uniform

One of the wondrous secrets of the Lowcountry is word-of-mouth advertising can be more powerful than paid advertising. Therefore, in twenty-three years I never once advertised myself looking for Santa events.

The events came to me.

There was never any intention on my part of wanting to become *The Santa to call.* I was content with the three annual events in which I participated. At one point, however, I was no longer just walking the streets of Beaufort, working Night On The Town and the parade in addition to Fripp Island and Cat Island.

The calls began, asking if Santa was available to work an event. The callers said they got my contact information from one of my three annual events...with the recommendation that my Santa was "the best ever", among other kind praises.

One of the earliest calls came from the Marine Corps Air Station in Beaufort. One of the squadrons, VMFA 333 (*Trip Tres*) needed a Santa for their Christmas party on the flight line, and their representative gave me a call. As the son of a career naval officer, I was honored to be invited to help the squadron celebrate Christmas. Santa was given a fire truck escort across the airfield, past fighter jets representing the best of America's airborne protectors. The families of the squadron's deployed personnel watched as Santa approached on that bright red 10-wheeled sleigh with flashing lights and sirens.

While on the subject of our Marine pilots, a few years later, during one Night On The Town event, Santa met two young girls who were waiting to visit St. Nick. They were in their early teens, wearing military flight jackets with the insignia of another local squadron. When it was their turn they came up and gently sat on Santa's knees. After a few normal welcoming comments and "Merry Christmas", Santa asked what the girls would like for Christmas.

They looked at each other, solidly knowing the answer. In turn, they both replied that all they wanted was a photo of them with Santa so they could send it to their father, who was stationed overseas. He wouldn't be home in time for Christmas.

Santa took extra time with the girls, posing in several photos so they would have a choice of many festive ones from which to choose.

The next year, the two girls came back to visit Santa at the Night On The Town event, and shared that the photos from the prior year arrived to their father in time for Christmas, and the photos were extremely popular in their father's camp...a small touch of Christmas at home for our military overseas.

Another Night On The Town visitor was a young girl, five or six years of age, who also had a special Christmas request. After her mother took several photos, Santa asked the little lady for her Christmas wishes. She replied, "When you're delivering presents on Christmas Eve, would you please take a few minutes to fly over my Daddy's camp in 'Ganistan' and make sure he's okay?"

"It'd be a pleasure to check on him for you," St. Nick replied. The little girl joyfully hugged Santa's neck, and bolted off to her family, ecstatic that she had somehow given her daddy a Christmas gift.

The following year, during Night On The Town, the same little girl greeted Santa with a huge smile. "Thank you for checking on Daddy! We kept our Christmas decorations up and had Christmas when he came home in February! Thank you!"

For our military and their families, and our first responders, nothing is more important than spreading cheer, joy, and faith during the Christmas season.

Santa Claus with members of the Beaufort Fire Department after a Christmas Parade

2001 - A Personal Loss

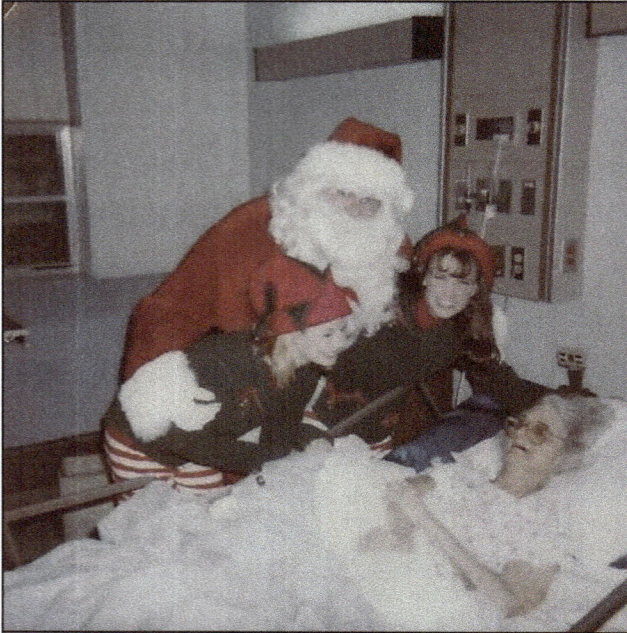

Personally, 2001 was the year I, and my family, suffered the first major personal loss of our own. After surviving a catastrophic stroke in 1983, which left her permanently bedridden and paralyzed on her right side, my mother passed away on Saint Patrick's Day 2001. The very last photo I took with Mom was when I visited her in the hospital in December 2000, dressed as Santa, with elves Julie (returning for one season) and Kelly accompanying me. A very special "thank you" goes to both young ladies, as Julie and Kelly also helped care for Mom in her apartment hospital bed all year!

In many respects, it was Mom's near-fatal stroke that changed my future, as I'd been exploring post-college job opportunities elsewhere in South Carolina. After her stroke, when we were gathered outside her room at the Medical University of South Carolina in Charleston, Dad told my brothers and me that we were to go live our lives and that he could take care of her, being the old experienced Navy Corpsman he was. However, I changed my plans and decided to stay in Beaufort.

But this particular visit, at Mom's bedside in Beaufort Memorial Hospital, was part of a larger one, as Santa and the elves also visited some children who were to spend Christmas in the hospital, and our visit brought many smiles to those sick kids. My mother, on a different floor, smiled at the colorful trio with the enthusiasm of a child herself...and something dawned on me. Santa not only brought cheer and joy to the young, but could also do so with the sick and elderly. This thought would gel within my mind for many months...

Once In A Lifetime

There was a very special "first-and-last" at the 2001 Night On The Town. My father never had his photo with Santa Claus, and in the first seven years when I walked in Santa's boots he was always home taking care of Mom. However, with her passing that year he was free to leave the apartment and finally see what Night On The Town was all about. He found Santa downtown, dressed down in a candy cane-patterned tunic and red suspenders to his red pants and black boots, as it was the warmest Night On The Town he ever had (and ever would, through 2015 at least). That night, my 70-year-old father sat on Santa's knee and smiled for his first and only photo with Saint Nick.

The author's father and Santa Claus, Night On The Town 2001

Elf in Training

Within the elf crew, Julie was ready to take off on her own ventures for good. Kelly welcomed a new rookie elf as Sami donned the red and green to help out with the children and families visiting Santa. Yes, this was the same Sami who, as a young girl, had asked for Santa to bring Frosty along and leave a little bit of himself on her floor Christmas morning. Sami never stopped believing in Santa!

A Special Request

At Night On The Town, Santa Claus received a special visit from an older couple with a unique request. They asked if Santa could come visit their home for Christmas. *(Santa Claus really can't be making Christmas Eve appearances because he's supposed to already be traveling across the world on Christmas Eve, delivering presents to boys and girls in all the countries!)*

This request, however, hit Santa in the heart. They were about to have their little granddaughter for Christmas for the last time. Her parents were divorcing and she was being taken to the West Coast to live. Santa agreed to visit, accompanied by elf Kelly, for a special Christmas visit, but a few days before December 24.

Kelly and Santa arrived at their front door well after the sun had gone down. He rang the bell, and waited a few seconds.

The grandfather opened the door, saying, "Well, look who's come to visit!" He called his granddaughter's name, and she came running from the living room...squealing in pure delight at the sight of Saint Nick and the green-clad elf!

It was a long visit, playing with that little girl, talking about school, her favorite toys and what she wanted to be when she grew up. There was no time limit on the visit, aside from when that dear little girl started to get tired. Santa rose and excused Kelly and himself, saying there were other children to visit before his Christmas Eve flight.

She got to her feet one more time, reaching up to Santa for one last hug before he left. Finally, the North Pole visitors made their way to the front door, and waiting there were the grandparents, tears of joy in their eyes.

It may have been their last Christmas visit with their granddaughter for many years, but it was a happy and memorable one...

Santa and Mama with Elf JT and staff
on Fripp Island 2001

"Santa Paws" and Sid

2001 was also the year I added another major Santa event: pet photos with St. Nick, known more popularly as "Santa Paws". It was a fundraiser for the Beaufort Humane Association (later Palmetto Animal League), and I was honored to become their "Santa Paws".

I love pets, and it was a great way to lift my spirits during that first Christmas Season without Mom. I think that God actually had a hand in this. Perhaps He knew it was time for Mom to

begin living life young and whole again at His side, and He would send me the gift of love from all manner of dogs and cats that show their affection whole-heartedly to those who naturally already love them.

The Santa Paws event was staged along Boundary Street in front of Kmart with either the fire department's 1957 Chevy firetruck or bucket truck Tower 1 as the big visual draw. Families brought dogs big and small, and cats, and any other personal pet, for that special photo with Santa.

Santa generated a lot of body heat in his suit, and the cats realized, once they got settled in his lap, that they were in a very warm, comfortable place to purr and sleep. Puppies were far more animated, not surprisingly, so some were happy to be held and others wanted Santa to sit with them on the ground.

Over the next twenty years Santa took photos with hundreds of pets at various events, loving each and every one as if they were all his own. One, however, not only didn't want to sit with Santa...he didn't want to be NEAR Santa!

That was Sid.

Sid was a magnificent, handsome, and well-muscled Mastiff, and didn't want to be anywhere close to Santa Claus! It would be more accurate to say that Sid was terrified of Santa.

The best photo taken was of huge Sid, pushing backwards away from Santa with his tail completely tucked between his legs, with his mommy holding him by the collar. Conversely, Sid's traveling companion was a little Yorkshire terrier who had no problem cuddling in Santa's arms!

"I am NOT sitting in your lap; I don't care how many bones you bring me for Christmas!" ~Sid

The author's puppy, Tasia, got her first photo with Santa in 2007!

Not Just For The Children...

The desire to spread as much Christmas cheer as possible led the Clauses to the River Oaks Assisted Living facility in Port Royal to visit the elderly who lived there with varying levels of care. Santa and Mrs. Claus arrived at dinner time to visit the residents who could move on their own, to the great enjoyment of all. No one was left out, however, as the Merry Couple went to the 24/7 care area and visited every remaining resident in their rooms or in their own social area. One gentleman was intubated in his room, unable to get up and barely able to lift his arms, but smiled happily upon seeing Santa and Mama enter his room to wish him a Merry Christmas. Several other bedridden residents beamed brightly as the Merry Couple visited each, holding their hands as requested, wishing them Christmas cheer and prayers.

They visited the next year, and that same gentleman was in the main dining hall, and after our "Merry Christmas" greeting he stopped Mrs. Claus when she passed his table, saying, "I want to apologize for last year. I couldn't get out of my bed when you visited me, but a gentleman is supposed to stand when a lady enters the room." He rose from his seat, took Mrs. Claus' hands in his, and said, "Merry Christmas, Mrs. Claus," as he bowed his head. A Christmas miracle!

One memorable beautiful lady in particular, Miss Betty, was seated in a wheelchair and when she saw Santa reached up her arms with tears of joy welling in her deep brown eyes. Her speech was very limited, but her happy cry of "Santa! Santa!" was as clear as a church bell. The Jolly Elf bent over so that she could give as strong a hug as she could from her seat, and he returned her hug warmly. "Santa! Santa!" she cried again happily. "I sorry I can't get up! But next year, next year, I gonna walk with you! I gonna walk with you!"

"And I will walk with you!" he said back in his deep bass. "Everyone will see us strolling together for Christmas!"

And when Santa and Mrs. Claus returned to visit in the next year…

…Miss Betty and Santa strolled the halls of River Oaks together, arm in arm, free from her wheelchair…another Christmas miracle!

Ten Years Already!

It only took ten years, but my Santa was finally and firmly established as The Event Santa to visit during the Beaufort Christmas Season (not to slight any other gents in their Red Suits, by the way). I had invested in multiple high-quality Claus outfits for Mendy and me for our daytime and nighttime appearances, and my own Santa hair and beard were of ultra-high quality and glued on with Hollywood-strength adhesives. No one had any trouble believing that Santa and Mama Claus were really married, and her career as a teacher the rest of the year gave her a natural rapport with the children who visited us. We were on our second set of young ladies as elves who worked with the children and their families to direct children to either Mrs. Claus or Santa (especially if any were suddenly too scared to visit Santa for fear of being found out that they'd been bad during the year!). Little girls would naturally flock to Mrs. Claus, little boys to Santa, and together all the Santa Family members actually sped up the time it took for waiting youngsters to visit. It had become normal for revelers to take photos with the elves, or with Mama, or with Santa, or any combination thereof.

Santa and Mrs. Claus with Rudolph and
Frosty on Fripp Island

Main Street Beaufort changed where Santa and company would be during Night On The Town. Since my first year as The Jolly Elf the crowd had grown from hundreds to over a thousand or more, and it was just getting impossible to meet with everyone in the middle of Bay Street and get through the crowd to the tree lighting on time. We were moved to rocking chairs under the Bay Street Clock at the entrance to the Waterfront Park, and the crowd organized itself into a line, allowing our elves to join us as seated guests awaiting the children.

"All I Want Is a Barbie"

There was one special little girl who wrote a heart-tugging letter. She and her family had very little, and all she asked for Christmas was a Barbie doll. Santa was so moved by her letter that he did indeed get her a brand-new Barbie...as well as Barbie-themed clothes, shoes, inflatable chair, blanket, and more. Mrs. Claus thought St. Nick went a little overboard, but that poor little girl deserved an incredible Christmas memory!

There's No Business Like "Show-Ho-Ho" Business

The year 2003 brought another venue for the Jolly Old Elf. The Beaufort Academy of Dance asked Santa to be part of its Christmas show! The plot of this show was Santa needed help finding a present for Mrs. Claus. During the performance he also introduced the academy's students of all ages for various dances. Mama Claus couldn't participate live, as the elves did need supervision at the North Pole that night, so she called in on stage via Santa's super-secret cell phone! The show ended with the young ladies, dressed as reindeer, pulling Santa across the stage in a custom-built sleigh, as he wished the audience a "Merry Christmas to all, and to all a good night!" After the show he met with children when they exited the theatre!

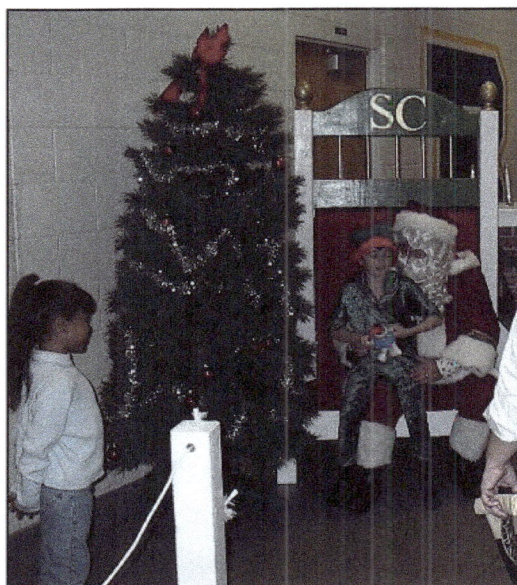

Proof!

Yes, boys and girls, Santa does get thirsty during his visits to the Lowcountry, especially when the local humidity and temperature are too high! After all, Santa does live in a magical snowy Workshop Complex at the North Pole. But, if there was any doubt about his favorite drink, Santa was caught on camera proving he only drinks The Real Thing!

"Can I Have Your Autograph, Santa?"

Occasionally a happy youngster wants more than just a photo with Santa and Mrs. Claus as a memory of his happy visit; he wants their autographs, too! The Merry Couple was only too happy to comply, along with a special personal message!

日本からメリークリスマス！ *

       Occasionally, someone can't wait for Santa to come to their country for a visit so they go to wherever Santa is appearing! This young lady came all the way from Japan to Beaufort, and timely was in the Spotted Dog (now ARTWorks in Beaufort Town Center) to get a picture with Santa and Mrs. Claus. This photo was well-circulated throughout her home country! It was a great pleasure to have met you, Kanoko!

*- "Merry Christmas From Japan!"

"Santa Paws" in the Studio

In 2005 Santa Claus traveled with the Beaufort Humane Association for a day of "Santa Paws" pet photos in Port Royal. It was a comfortable day out of the weather with many happy pets visiting Santa!

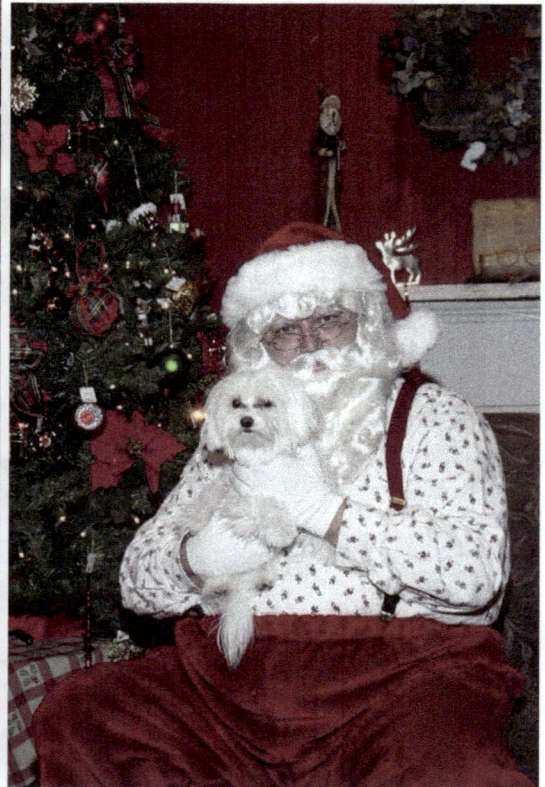

Photos by Brett Byers, Port Royal Photograhy & Custom Framing, 2005

from the author's photo collection

There's No Business Like "Snow-Ho-Ho" Business

Beaufort is a beautiful, historic southern city, nestled along the Beaufort River on the Intracoastal Waterway. Directly south from the Waterfront Park one can see Parris Island Marine Corps Recruit Depot at the point where the Beaufort River and Battery Creek meet on their way to the Atlantic Ocean. During Christmastime we do see a lot of colorful lights and decorations.

What we don't get much of here is snow.

In 2005 the city decided to change that. Thus was conceived *Blizzard On the Bay*.

An ice truck was brought in, along with a grinder, to create a few dozen square feet of cold man-made snow on the grounds across from the Best Western, beside the city Christmas tree. Santa was invited to talk with children after they'd had some playtime in the artificial drifts. It was quite the entertaining warm day of people in short sleeves and children shivering in snow-filled delight!

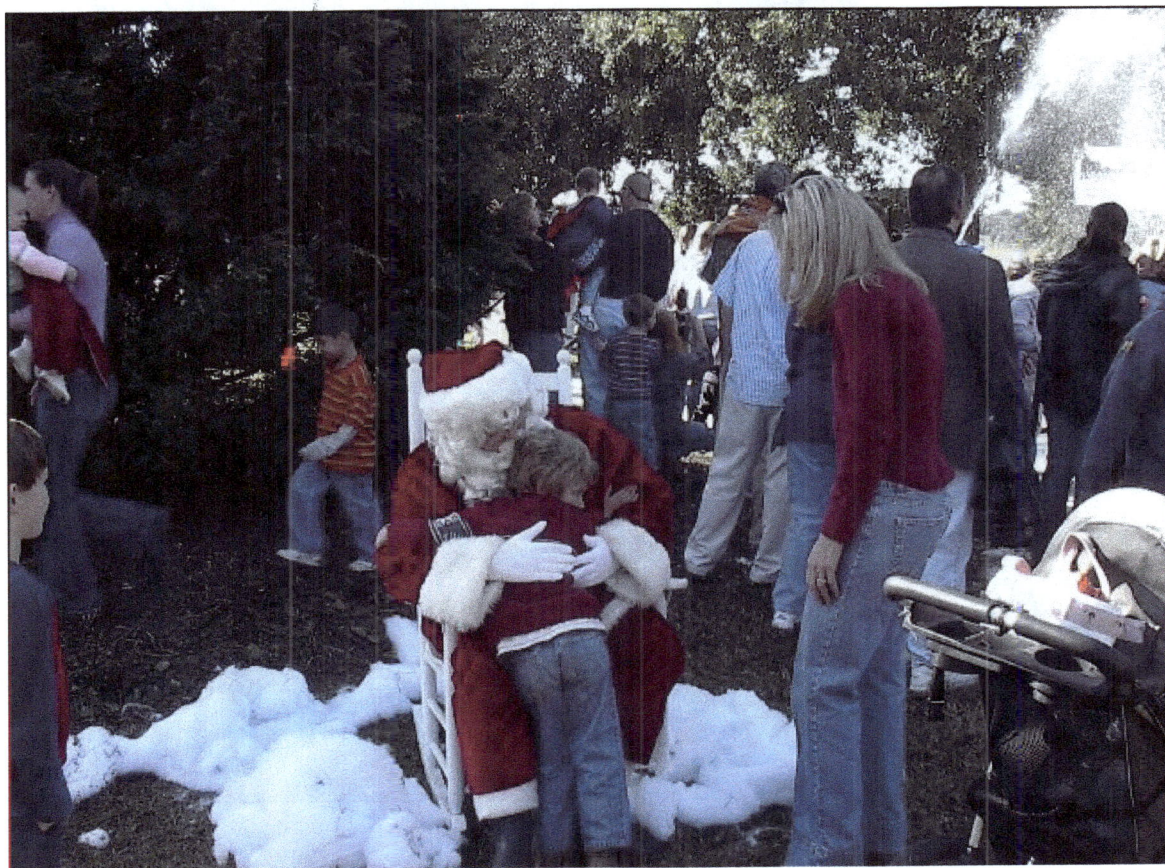

A very cool visit with Santa Claus!

A New View on Fripp Island

Santa became a film star on Fripp Island in 2005, as he and Mrs. Claus filmed their first promo video for residents and guests on the island. It took a few takes, but the Jolly Couple nailed it as part of Fripp Island's holiday welcome video.

Screen capture from 2005 Christmas Greeting on Fripp Island Cable

Warm temperatures, however, didn't keep Santa and Mama from enjoying the beauty of Fripp Island. There was a little extra time in that year's *Breakfast with The Clauses*, giving them a while to stroll along the beach, enjoying the serenity of Fripp Island's coastline.

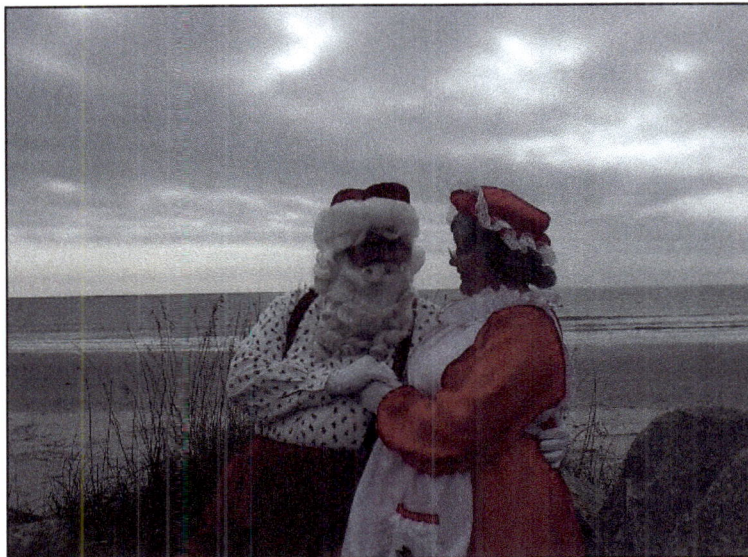

It quickly became a tradition to take a photo with Santa and Mama Claus in the morning with the beautiful Atlantic Ocean in the background.

Another Breakfast With Santa!

In 2005 Santa added another short-term annual visit: the MOMS of Beaufort Baptist Church invited him and Mrs. Claus to a Saturday breakfast to visit their families and children. He was set up in The Green Room on a festively-decorated stage where the children could visit after eating and take photos with the Jolly Old Elf!

𝔑ight 𝔒n 𝔗he 𝔗own - 𝔜ou𝔗ube 𝔐ovie

In 2006 a Beaufort resident loaded a video of Night On The Town to YouTube (https://www.youtube.com/watch?v=73Hsdb2KRSM). It lasts only a couple of minutes, but you might catch a glimpse of a white-bearded old gent in a red suit lighting the Beaufort Christmas Tree.

Santa appears at the 2:10 mark of this video, with a little extra Kringle moment: In the Christmas Story Santa is seen with the "stump of a pipe" in his teeth, with the pipe smoke circling his head "like a wreath". Well, if you ever attended Night On The Town, you might have seen Santa with a lit pipe in his teeth as he pantomimed Santa's actions in the story. Political correctness was not part of Santa's character as he puffed on his pipe and North Pole tobacco…and not one person out of the thousands at Night On The Town ever complained all the years he appeared with pipe in hand…er, teeth! But, as a courtesy to everyone, this was the only time Santa ever smoked his pipe in public.

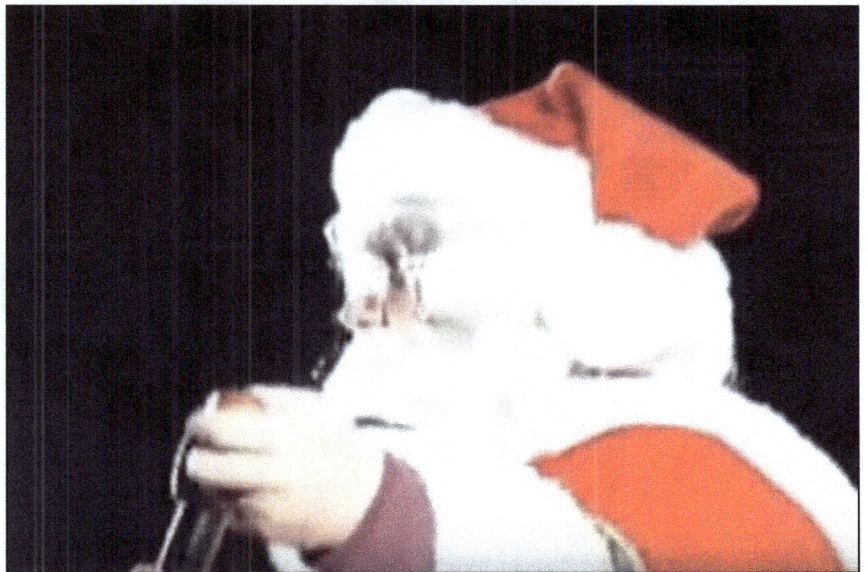

No "Palmetto Bluff" -ing

I received an invitation from a lady who had worked with Santa and Mama Claus at Fripp Island; she was now working at Palmetto Bluff in Bluffton and asked if I could bring the Clauses for a Christmastime visit. I said, "Yes, of course!" We had a beautiful outdoor venue with centuries-old tabby ruins for the background. This was an absolutely gorgeous Christmas photo setting. (www.palmettobluff.com)

A Port Royal Grand Opening

A new retail area opened n Port Royal in 2006 called "The Village", a group of small stores set up on Paris Avenue not far from the current wildlife viewing porch and Post Office.

Santa was invited to help inaugurate the opening of the new stores, along with singers dressed in Victorian finest, and took many photos with visitors at Port Royal's newest stores. It was quite a surprise to Port Royal residents to see Santa on Paris Avenue that December Friday evening, waving to them as they passed by!

𝔖aint 𝔑icholas—the 𝔖equel

I serve as a lay minister at St. Peter's Catholic Church in Beaufort, which added the spirit to being a "Christian" Santa as opposed to a "retail" Santa. My Santa openly prayed with children or adults who wanted to do so, and again my Santa always greeted with "Merry Christmas" and often offered "God Bless You", and never in my entire career did Santa say, "Happy Holidays". Not once did anyone complain about my Santa's religious interaction with his child visitors. I was asked by my pastor in 2006 and 2007 to attend our church's *Breakfast with Santa*, to which I gladly accepted. My Santa felt at home as Saint Nicholas' modern namesake with our Parish's youngsters, and again the children equally divided between Santa and Mama Claus when they came to visit. They eagerly talked about school, toys they wanted for Christmas and much more. Many times some would "tattletale" on their brothers and sisters, in hope that Santa would place them on the naughty list!

Our Parish had built a new house of worship next to the old one, which became the new Walsh Palmetto Room, and the staff certainly decorated it in true Christmas cheer.

Another Night On The Town Move

As the years passed at Night On The Town, the crowds got bigger and the lines got longer, but in a festive sense, of course! The decision was made in 2007 to move Santa and Mama Claus, now without elves, back into the Old Bay Marketplace for the night's Santa visit and photos.

They were located next to the elevator that led to the second floor of the building, and was decorated quite nicely to welcome the Merry Couple! This is where Santa would be found every year from then on...

"Branch" -ing Out

Another one of those perfect-photo moments came in 2007 as Santa and Mama were making their way toward Bay Street and Night On The Town. A store on Port Republic Street, *Branches* (unfortunately no longer there), had decorated the entire store with Christmas trees and presents from wall to wall. The Merry Couple stepped inside to visit and admire it all, and were able to take some great photos together. They felt as though they were home in their own North Pole Workshop Greenhouse.

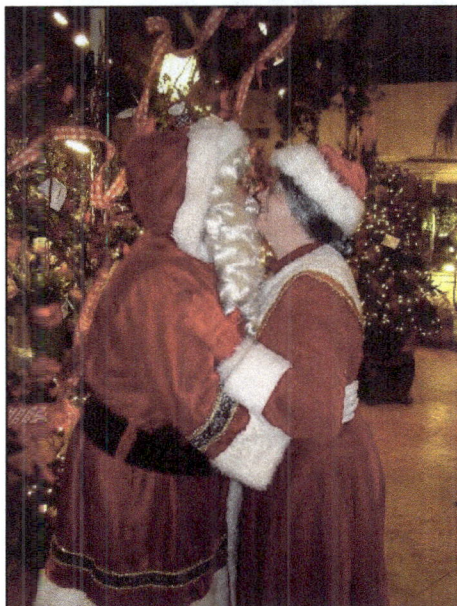

"Straight Talk with Santa"

Saint Nick was interviewed prior to his 2008 Christmas Eve flight by Cathy Harley of *The Beaufort Gazette*. For the first time boys and girls were able to learn a little about Santa's secrets of Christmas! The following conversation appeared in the December 23, 2008 *Gazette*.

© The Beaufort Gazette

December 23 2008 Staff Photo by Bob Sofaly

Santa Claus has been spotted around the Lowcountry for the past several months playing with trains and riding in the Beaufort Fire Department's big Tower 1 Truck.

In an exclusive interview with The Beaufort Gazette, Claus shares his top-secret information on his busiest night of the year.

Q. What are some of the most popular new toys children in Beaufort have been asking for this year?

A. Ho-ho-ho. The most popular toy this year reminds me of France, where I am known as Papa Noel…the Wii. (Get it? "Oui"? It's a Santa joke.) Aside from that, there have been many requests for games and toys based on "The Dark Knight" and "Star Wars" and "Iron Man"… and the always-requested Power Rangers. And let's not forget the ever-popular American Girl dolls, too. Recent new favorites the past couple Christmas seasons have been the Webkins and MP3 players…and many, many, many children are asking for their own laptops (some actually want them for studying, too).

Q. What are some of the old favorite toys that children are requesting?

A. I'm never disappointed by the number of Barbie's and baby dolls that little girls would like as presents, and makeup kits and Easy Bake Ovens, and the little boys do still ask for G.I. Joe's and trucks (lots and lots of dump trucks and fire trucks) and baseballs and gloves and footballs and roller skates and skateboards.

© The Beaufort Gazette

December 23 2008 Staff Photo by Bob Sofaly

Q. Are there any humorous remarks or requests you have received from children?

A. I am always surprised and amused when a good little boy or girl here ask for ice skates when we visit Beaufort County…makes me wonder if my official weather elf, Ferdinand de North-Pole, knows something about the upcoming weather he hadn't passed on. I'm often asked for rich husbands or wives; those are always challenging, and I call my good friend Cupid for help with those special requests.

Q. What toys do YOU like to play with and why? Do you try some of them out when you deliver them?

A.I have 11 months of the year to test the new toys built at the workshop and commit those toys and their various versions to memory, so that when a young girl or boy is describing their wishes, or reading their lists to me, I know exactly which toy in my inventory is just right to deliver to her or him. But, there's no playing or testing the toys on The Night. There are far too many miles to travel to spend time testing at every house…I trust all my wonderful elves to make sure each and every gift is in perfect condition when opened on Christmas morning.

© The Beaufort Gazette

December 23 2008 Staff Photo by Bob Sofaly

Q. You have had many appearances in the Lowcountry this year and in years past, do you have a favorite place?

A. There's no one place in particular, as ALL of the Lowcountry is my favorite. Ms. Claus and I do particularly enjoy our Saturday mornings on Fripp Island as we take photos with the children and their families with the beach in the background…and we also enjoy all the wonderful boys and girls and their families at the fabulous *Night On The Town*. *Night On The Town* is like Christmas Eve…the time just seems to go so quickly, and yet we get to visit with dozens and dozens of terrific children in that time, surrounded by such natural and decorated beauty. Every place we go is so very special, and Mama and I have many years of fond memories of the Lowcountry that only grow in number as the years pass.

Q. Do you ever get to visit us during the summer for fishing and sunbathing? We imagine you have a secret hideout in the area.

A. Oh, trust me when I say, I return to the Lowcountry quite often. However, in order to not attract attention during our off-season, Mama and I travel "in-Claus-nito"…Hc-ho-ho! (We are always here during Water Festival so you better watch out.)

Q. What is it like to ride in Tower 1, the biggest fire truck with the Beaufort Fire Department? It seems so high up there. How does it compare to riding in your sleigh?

A. Tower 1 is much like riding in North Pole 1. (We have several sleighs, and North Pole 1 is the most comfortable and sturdiest, and is the one used every Dec. 24. The others are used mostly for reindeer training exercises and a little navigation practice for ole' St. Nick, too.) Both are built very sturdy, with compactly built operating controls so as to allow the pilot the most control with minimum effort and lots of room for carrying all those presents. But the big difference is North Pole 1 has state-of-the-art GPS systems that are also connected with NORAD (be sure to check out their site on Christmas Eve, and you can follow me all across the world on high-resolution radar images). And, to help me stay on time, a very special countdown clock for the 24 Earth-time hours of present delivery across this beautiful globe we all call home.

Q. What is your favorite snack to eat on Christmas Eve?

A. Hmmm…I'd have to say…chocolate chip cookies.

Q. How many calories do you consume in a Christmas night?

A. I read this year in The North Pole Times that Michael Phelps has a 30,000-calorie daily diet. Well, that would get me through Beaufort, Port Royal, Lady's Island, St. Helena Island, all the way out to Fripp and across the rest of the upper half of Beaufort County. My special thanks to that nice couple in Mossy Oaks who leave me that nice hot chocolate-flavored coffee with the cookies every year. (I'll let you figure the calorie math after that, and you tell me what you come up with when I come back next Christmas season.)

Q. How do you know who should be on the Naughty or Nice list?

A. Moms and dads have that super-secret special way to notify the N&N ("Naughty and Nice") Central Command at the North Pole. And, of course, we do have our elves among the boys and girls keeping an eye on them in person all through the year -- "in-Claus-nito," of course.

(This last answer was before I had ever heard of an "Elf on the Shelf"…and before I added a very important accessory many years later!)

A Revised Breakfast Visit

Santa decided during the 2008 *Breakfast with The Clauses* on Fripp Island that he and Mama would visit the families while they dined in the Fripp Island Beach Club.

The children were excited by the unscheduled visit while they ate delicious and healthy breakfasts. Even though there were photos taken at the breakfast table, they could also go upstairs to visit Santa and Mama for a more formal morning visit and photo.

A Jolly Grand Opening

A new Holiday Inn hotel was built here in Beaufort in 2009, and Santa was invited to attend the Grand Opening. There was a grand dinner inside the hotel and Santa helped deliver presents to the attendees in the ballroom.

At the end of the evening was the official ribbon-cutting to open the hotel to the public, and Santa Claus was among the dignitaries as part of the ceremony!

Photos courtesy Rose Ewing

Dressing a Little Casual for the Parade, Santa?

The Beaufort Christmas Parade in 2009 saw Santa and Mama in different outfits than they wore the last several years. This was due to the weather at Night On The Town the previous Friday, December 4. It lightly rained during the evening, the first time that happened in all my Santa years. As sturdy as our expensive Santa suits were, they were unfortunately delicate to the effects of water. Both outfits were severely water-damaged after two hours in the drizzle. Without time available to repair and clean them for Sunday, we instead wore an equally-high quality pair of Santa suits that matched each other but lacked the fancy gold trim on the hems. They didn't look the same as the prior year, but the waving style and cheerful greeting by Santa and Mama to the crowds along Boundary, Carteret, and Bay Streets told everyone this was the same Mama and Santa, and he wore the same massive mistletoe-engraved belt buckle. That was the only year Santa would be dressed-down since first wearing his Old-World-Style brocade for so many years. However, he was back in his dress-up suit in 2010.

That's why Santa had several suits…always prepared for the worst.

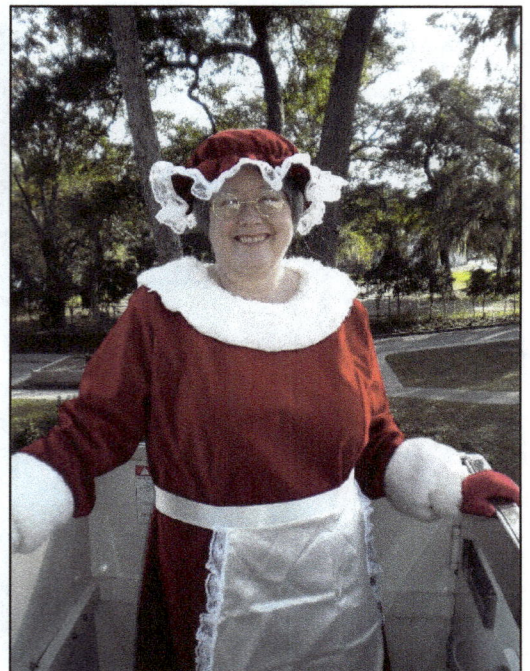

Did you know from Santa and Mama's vantage point, they could watch the parade themselves? No better way to watch a parade than from twenty feet high!

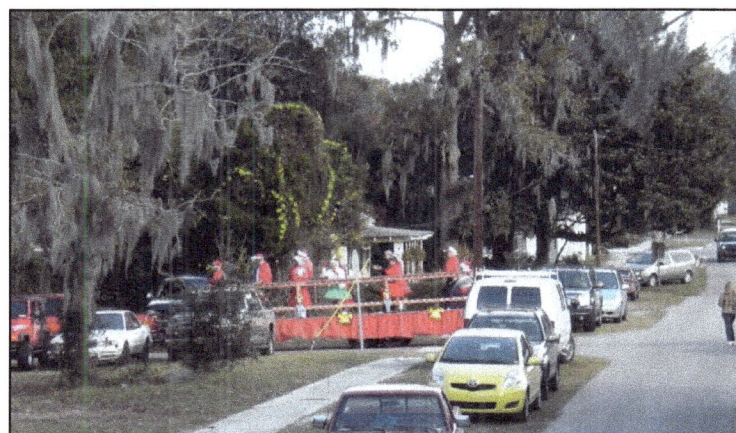

The Return of The Elf

There was a several-year period in which only Santa and Mama appeared in the Christmas visits to Beaufort. In 2010 Kelly, Santa's second elf, returned after many years. Her character's story was that she'd grown up into the role of the Elf On the Shelf, Poinsettia. (Recall from Santa's Gazette interview that I'd never heard of an "Elf On the Shelf", and she had to explain the concept when she came back to the Santa Family.) She designed her new elf suit, and when she wore it she looked like an actual Shelf Elf! Poinsettia joined Santa and Mama for the entire 2010 Christmas Season, starting at Fripp Island and continuing into Main Street's Christmas Weekend of Night On The Town and the Christmas Parade. The extra help was appreciated because of the ever-growing crowd of visitors at major events.

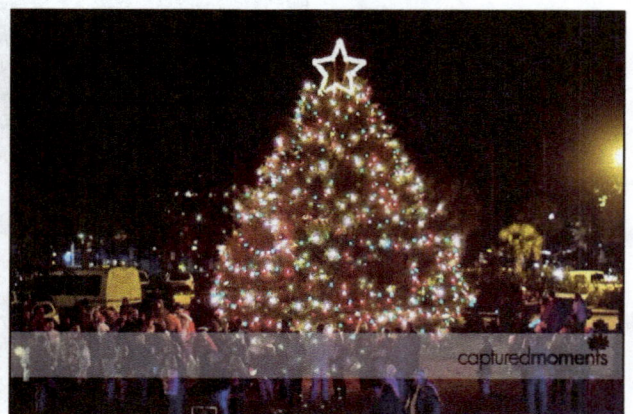

Photos courtesy Captured Moments Photography

www.cmoments.com

Santa Bits and Pieces

In addition to the operating motto *Maintain the Reality of the Illusion*, the Santa Family had another equally-important rule: *No One Leaves Unhappy*. That meant Santa and Mama and the Elves did whatever it took to make the photo moment the best ever.

Santa and Mama often took "breaks" whenever a child was not at all interested to be put on Santa's knee, or even for Mrs. Claus or an Elf to hold him or her. In those situations, Santa rose from the chair and offered the parent to let the child sit in Santa's chair alone, which always got approval. The child watched the Merry Ones walk away from the chair. When the little one's attention was finally redirected back to the family and photographer, Santa and Mama would circle around to hide behind the chair and secretly pop out to make the magic happen and create the "happy child with Santa" photo memory.

Occasionally a precious toddler not only didn't want to sit on Santa's lap, but changed the gravitational constant of the universe around him and dropped to the floor, refusing to be moved toward Santa. So, Saint Nick would climb down to the floor to the entertainment and laughter of everyone watching the humorous scene to take photos of children and him playing together on the floor, sometimes nearly nose to nose!

Santa Claus, of course, loved to take photos with pets, and it didn't matter what kind of pet: dogs, cats, rabbits, turtles, snakes, birds, lizards...if it was someone's pet, Santa was honored to hold it and have fun. One cold "Santa Paws" day a few small black kittens were brought to Santa for a promo photo to find them homes; they found a home, all right...they buried themselves in his beard and purred themselves to sleep. Ferrets loved to run up his arms and into his hat, to show they were on top of the world! Santa, of course, speaks fluent *animal* at all times and could receive all their Christmas wishes as well, including bones and toy mice and birdseed...although the tarantulas' present requests were a challenge to fill! Dogs were always excited to be with Saint Nick: the little ones were generally hyper and agile, the large ones tried to run and play. They didn't remember Santa handles nine full-size reindeer every Christmas Eve so they weren't going to get away that easily!

Always honored to help spread Christmas cheer and spirit, Santa often went to churches and schools to waiting excited children and families, to bring smiles to disabled children, adults and the elderly, and even deliver cheer and hope to cancer patients undergoing active chemo treatment. No one was forgotten, all were equally treasured, and the love of God was shared with each and every one. Sometimes...that's all someone needs.

The Return of "Santa Paws"

Santa and Poinsettia were invited to repeat *Santa Paws* with the Palmetto Animal League (formerly Beaufort Humane Association) in its new location on Okatie Highway in Ridgeland, South Carolina.

Poinsettia and Santa were perfectly at ease with all the pets that came to visit: dogs, cats, birds, ferrets, whichever wanted to visit Santa…they were all warmly welcomed. Here are a few adorable moments from the 2010 *Santa Paws* event. The links below are to the videos taken of the two years at the Okatie facility, or one can simply search for Palmetto Animal League at YouTube.com to find these videos…they are absolutely adorable!

Santa Paws 2010 PAL https://www.youtube.com/watch?v=IUAg5fU-EmQ

Santa Paws 2012 PAL https://www.youtube.com/watch?v=vO59pKCKciQ

Breakfast With Santa, Chick-Fil-A Style

In 2010 Santa had a new annual appearance at Beaufort's Chick-Fil-A on Boundary Street. He was invited to their *Breakfast with Santa* event, and the setup was more relaxed than dressy. Santa enjoyed the appearance in his more comfortable outfit (candy cane tunic and suspenders or overalls). The event proved to be a hit for Chick-Fil-A, and Santa was booked for the next year immediately…and every year after, the customer crowd was bigger than the prior year! Beaufort photographer Todd Stowe was behind the camera (except 2015), and all of them can be seen on his website www.toddstowe.com.

Photos courtesy Todd Stowe Photography

www.toddstowe.com

Photos courtesy Todd Stowe Photography

www.toddstowe.com

Back to the Bluff

Santa was invited to Palmetto Bluff in 2010 for a private property owners' outdoor party, so while there Santa and Poinsettia explored the beautiful grounds. Where else would you find Saint Nick and an elf in a tree house?

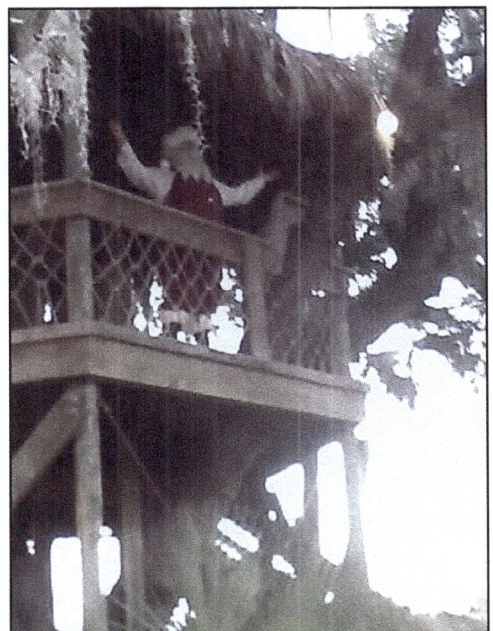

"Mrs. Claus Is Watching the Elves"

My wife moved to a new teaching position at Beaufort Elementary School, and we decided together that Mrs. Claus would retire from Beaufort-centered events so that students at her new school would not recognize her in the red dress and salt-and-pepper wig and ask why she was pretending to be Santa's wife. Her appearances each year were limited to Fripp Island only beginning in 2011 until 2015.

She did not disappear from Santa events completely, however. Dennis Adams, the Beaufort librarian who for years read the Christmas Story at Night On The Town, retired from the Christmas event after 2009. The 2010 Night On The Town was the only one during which the Christmas Story was not read.

Santa Claus and Beaufort County Librarian Dennis Adams

Night On The Town just didn't feel right without the Story being read, so I approached Main Street and proposed that since Mendy could not appear as Mrs. Claus anymore that she, as a Beaufort Elementary teacher, do it instead. It was approved, and Mendy took over that position in 2011. No one recognized her as having been Mrs. Claus for so many years, so her taking over the story reading was seamless, and worked well.

Mendy reading the Christmas Story 2011 Night On The Town

Mayor Billy Keyserling and Santa Claus, 2011 Night On The Town

Photos courtesy Captured Moments Photography

www.cmoments.com

Beaufort author Kim Poovey filled in for the 2014 reading of the Christmas Story

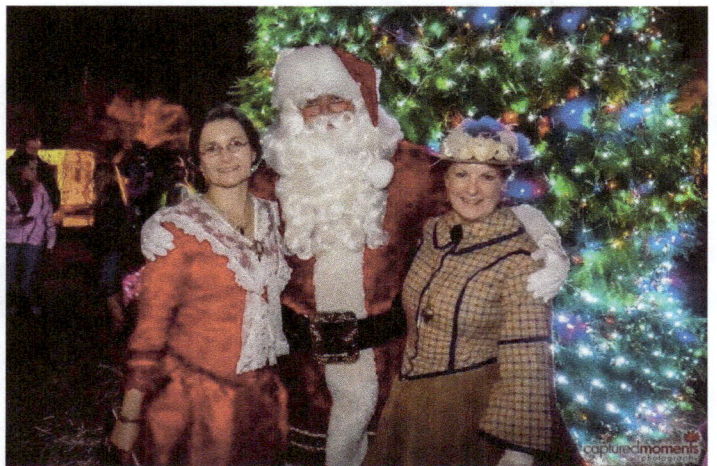

Santa with Kim Poovey and Lynn Bristow Cook of South Carolina Lowcountry Tourism

Photos courtesy Captured Moments Photography

www.cmoments.com

A Special Reunion...and a Christmas Surprise!

The year 2011 was also the year that I was reunited with my high school best friend, Cyndi Williams-Barnier, after thirty-two years, and we started our high-school dream of writing together. If you've ever visited us at one of our book signings or author events, you may have heard us talk about how we got together decades after high school graduation and began writing the books we talked about. We reconnected and caught up on each other's lives. We discovered that many times over the years we were within feet of each other and never knew it...including Santa events. She, of course, would not have recognized me because of the heavy makeup I wore in the Red Suit. Nor did she know that the Santa waving at her and her children, Mandy and Justin, from the '57 fire truck, and later the bucket of Tower 1, was I.

In 2014 she decided to put up a Christmas tree in her home for the first time n years (with some thanks due to her partner working as Beaufort's Santa Claus). While plundering within the attic she discovered something she had forgotten about for fifteen years...a photo of her son and daughter with Santa Claus. She called me on her cell phone from the attic. "I found a photo of you with my kids! I recognize the eyes!"

"Send me a pic of it!" I said. The photo was from a day when I was posing for Santa photos at the former Boombears in Beaufort. Another family member had taken her children for the photo shoot, so I didn't cross paths with Cyndi that day.

That photo is included here, and remains on display year-round in her home, no longer buried in the attic.

During the 2011 Night On The Town, Cyndi finally had her first photo with the very same Santa she and her children used to wave to during the annual Christmas Parades, but this time knowing exactly who was under The Red Suit.

Photo courtesy Captured Moments Photography

www.cmoments.com

Capturing the Christmas Moments

After thirteen years, studio photos with Santa returned when Captured Moments Photography opened up for business in Beaufort. Eric and Susan Smith worked digital photography to amazing ends, creating imagery beyond anything I'd ever seen. When they were looking for a Santa for their first Christmas studio photos they were given only one recommendation by the community: yes, that was I. They built a beautiful Christmas stage for children to take photos with Santa, and it was with Captured Moments that we created the "Peek-A-Boo" pose. Santa would hide behind the set curtains when a child was less than happy about sitting with Santa. On cue by Eric, Santa would pop out from behind the curtain to make a surprise appearance in the photo without the child any the wiser. These photos were some of the most fun and creative in which I'd ever participated.

One photo in particular involved two little boys. After Eric had finished taking the photos for the customer's photo package, he turned the boys' grandmother to show her some of the photos on his camera's screen. The boys, identical twins, decided they weren't finished visiting with Santa, and instead of joining their grandmother they turned back to Santa and began peppering him with question after question about the North Pole and the reindeer and Mrs. Claus and the elves and on and on. Eric turned to see that scene and immediately began taking more photos.

One of those photos is the cover of this book.

And those twin boys are the sons of elf Kelly / Poinsettia.

Photos courtesy Captured Moments Photography

www.cmoments.com

116

Helena Place

A new annual appearance was created through a personal connection from my church, Saint Peter's Catholic Church on Lady's Island. One of my fellow parishioners, Rose, had worked with me at other events through my earlier years at Fripp Island, Cat Island, Holiday Inn, and so on. She was now the manager of the Helena Place Assisted Living in Port Royal and invited me to bring Santa to visit the residents.

There was much joy when Santa visited the elderly. Many were mentally receding from the present, and were as excited as children when that white-bearded old elf arrived. His voice bellowed when necessary so they could hear him, and all were smiling. Santa wished them Christmas blessings and prayers at each visit.

One resident in particular meant the most to the man under the Red Suit. I'd mentioned before that I serve at St. Peter's Catholic Church here in Beaufort. Jimi Savarese, who had served on the church's Liturgical Committee, recommended me to succeed her when she retired from active church service and moved into Helena Place. She was the only Helena Place resident who knew who was under that huge white beard. Santa always greeted her last on his way out when his visit was complete. She would whisper, "You are a beautiful Santa! Bless you for coming to visit us…"

The honor was all mine, Jimi…and Santa's, too. Rest in peace, lovely lady…

Santa Claus handing out Christmas Presents

Santa with Dottie McDaniel

Santa with Essie Bishop

Santa with Theresa Reed

All too often Santa's visit was the highlight of a final Christmas...before they joined our Lord in heaven.

They will always be remembered...

Santa chatting with former Beaufort County Councilman and Treasurer Eldrid Moody

Santa with Vera Black

Santa with Gail Hodsdon

...and Santa gets a "thank you" for another Christmas well-done!

Helena Place photos courtesy Rose Ewing

My Wish List

Dear Santa:

I want a Pool,

Your Friend,

Cloey

Cloey knew just what to ask for as a Beaufort-area Christmas present in 2005!

miny ipod

Gift cards to
target
toys-r-us

Limid too
~~Gap~~

Stuffud animalls

C.D.s

sewing thing:

~~Luu~~
fur real friend
luv cubs ~~puppies~~
~~puppy~~ kittens

a t.v.

a DUPpla

Sometimes what a child really wants requires very close reading…from 2005

127

Part 4

Adaptation Claus

A Necessary New Accessory

When Santa and Mama Claus arrived on Fripp Island to launch the 2012 Christmas season, Santa was seen walking with a new accessory: a candy-cane style walking cane. It was a perfect fit with his old-world style brocade and personality, but it served a more important task.

In the spring of 2012 I suffered an event which caused my legs to stop working. While the details are unnecessary here, the result was that I never fully regained the use of my left leg and would be required from that point to walk with a cane. Santa, however, is immortal and can never be seen as anything less than perfect to the masses of children waiting to see him every Christmas season, so Santa couldn't be seen walking with a medical cane. I did have a full list of appearances lined up for 2012 and I didn't want to disappoint either the children or the event managers.

After much online searching, Santa did end up with a medical cane that would support his weight (almost 300 pounds in 2012) and look festive…The Candy-Cane Cane!

My research showed me that many Santas across the world had been using that same supportive device in their appearances, and it was perfect in their photos. It even came with its own legend: Santa could use it to determine if a child was good or bad simply by touching its handle to a child's forehead. So, the first time Saint Nick here was asked about the new cane, that was the reply he gave…and suddenly he had a couple dozen children waiting to be touched by Santa's Naughty-Or-Nice Magic Cane (*glad I didn't know about this back when Santa did that Beaufort Gazette interview!*). I only did it that one time, however, as I saw just how fast that became the go-to thing for children and didn't want to tempt fate with some little one accidentally pulling the cane to his forehead faster than I wanted. That request never came up again, and for the rest of the 2012 season, and the next three Christmas seasons, Santa's cane simply became seen as a decorative wardrobe accessory.

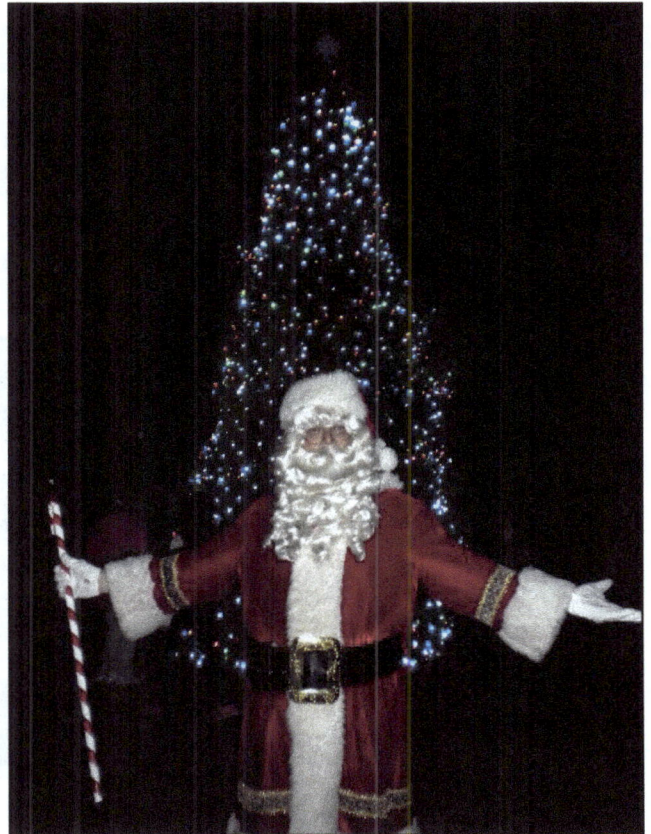

Santa's new cane also became a great way to lead the crowd of revelers in lighting the city Christmas tree at Night On The Town. It was difficult to see Santa when one was deep in the crowd, but that three-foot wooden red-and-white striped cane was visible no matter where one stood, and I could balance myself primarily on one leg for the time it took for me to lead the crowd in the tree-lighting countdown.

Poinsettia, the Elf On the Shelf, returned from the North Pole to join Santa for that year's Christmas Parade. Her appearance was out of need as I was having difficulty maintaining balance in the bucket of Tower 1 whenever it sped up or slowed down during the event. I had to place myself in one spot, so I wasn't able to wave to both sides of the street, as I had ever since Santa was first placed in Tower 1 years before. Poinsettia took care of waving to people on the left side and Santa on the right. Careful observers would have noticed starting that season that Santa never again moved from side to side in Tower 1's bucket, but remained fixed in one spot as he waved to the crowds.

Photos courtesy Captured Moments Photography

www.cmoments.com

130

© Captured Moments Photography

Photos courtesy Captured Moments Photography

www.cmoments.com

A New Breakfast With Santa

Lowcountry Produce Market and Cafe, a new restaurant in Beaufort, brought in Santa for the first time for a Breakfast with Santa event.

It was an enjoyable new photo-opportunity for people who missed the studio photo session at Captured Moments, and Santa was relaxed in his gold-buttoned red workshop overalls and candy-cane pattern tunic.

Page Photos from Lowcountry Produce Market and Cafe Facebook Page

Parris Island

When my father was stationed on Parris Island, I was attending military school in Virginia. I had a certain level of freedom when I visited, especially while in uniform, and more so when I had an officer's braid on my military cap. I was very proud when my father took me to visit the commanding general, play on the golf course (and I never did lose that wicked right-slice no matter how long I played), bowl in the bowling alley, shop in the PX, and more. Even during my newspaper years, I had fairly easy access to the base with my newspaper ID and bundles of papers in the back seat. 9/11 changed all that, and the couple of times I went to the base after the attack required me to be pulled over and my car inspected from stem to stern.

So, I had a lot of reticence when I was asked to do my first Santa appearance on the Marine Corps Recruit Depot. The image in my head was of me pulled to the side again, my luggage removed from the car to be inspected and dressed as Santa, I'd be on display for everyone to see as they passed through the main gate.

I was hired by MCCS to bring Santa to the new family welcome center to celebrate its opening and first Christmas season. My Santa uniform required two large travel bags, filling the front seat of my little red car (well, of course Santa drives a red car when he doesn't have his red sleigh!).

I had a great deal of trepidation driving to the Parris Island main gate for the first time in many years…but I was ready, and had my driver's license and new Santa Claus business card in hand. I was intentionally early in case I was to be inspected, expecting it might take ten or fifteen minutes to search my little car and the secret clothes in my bags.

My car rolled to a stop at the gate and a young marine approached. The guard asked where I was going and what my business on base was. I presented both my cards and said calmly, "I'm Santa Claus, and I have an event at MCCS housing."

I prepared to turn right to the inspection shack; the guard looked at my license, the Santa card, then at me…he handed them back, gave me a salute and a smile and said, "Merry Christmas, sir!" He waved me through to the causeway leading to Horse Island. I returned the salute with, "Merry Christmas to you, and thank you for your service, sir!"

God Bless our men and women in uniform…

Santa Sighting in Ridgeland

Santa Claus loves visiting churches, in keeping with his true Christian roots! He made a visit to Saint Paul's Methodist Church in Ridgeland to spread some Christmas cheer with the good folks in Jasper County's largest city!

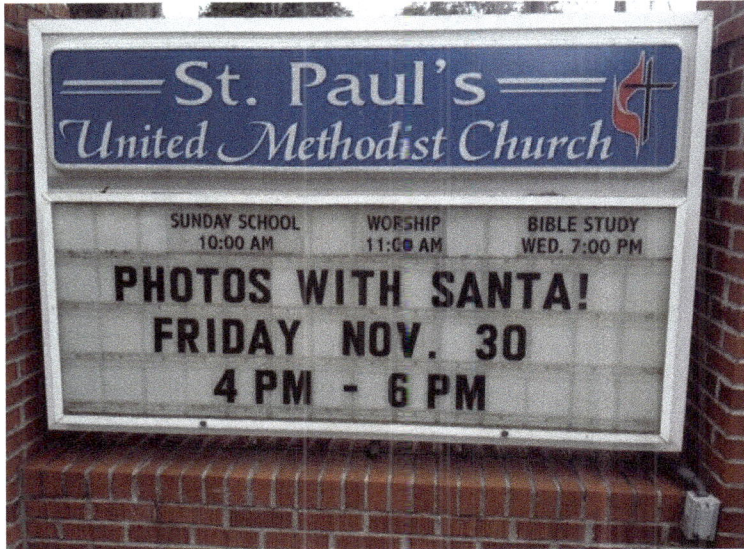

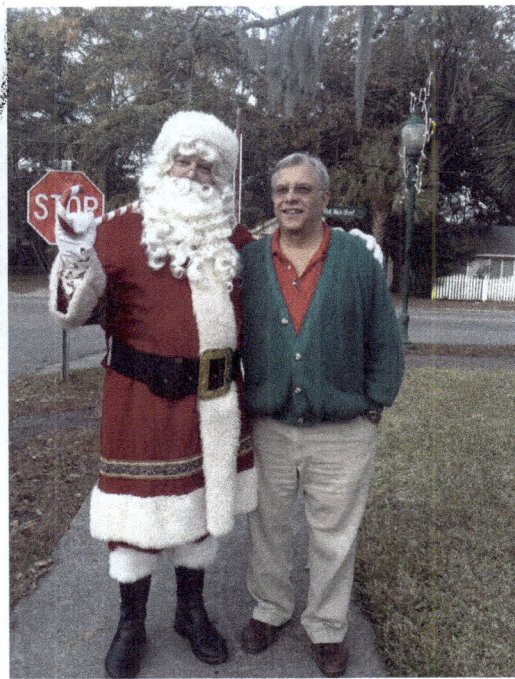

Santa with Beth Gregory and Bill Barnier of St. Paul's United Methodist Church

Santa Sighting in Beaufort

Even though Santa's busy appearance schedule kept him going to event after event, he never forgot what his main job was every Christmas season: visit with children! Some lucky youngsters caught him during a relaxing walk in downtown Beaufort!

Surf-ing into Beaufort Town Center

Beaufort Town Center, where Kmart has been located for decades, held its first Christmas community event. Santa was there to inaugurate it with local radio station 104.9 The Surf. A beautiful seating area was set up under the pergola in the middle of the parking lot, where Santa met with children, surrounded by brilliant red poinsettias. Santa even had a live radio interview with the station's on-site personality. At the end of the event, Santa did not take off in his reindeer-led sleigh, but in a fishing boat hauled by a great white pickup truck into the far shadows of Town Center!

The Show-Ho-Ho Goes On Once More!

Santa returned in another Christmas show for the Beaufort Academy of Dance! This show was about a young child who sneaks onto Santa's sleigh and goes to the North Pole, where she is discovered and is given a tour of all the incredible and beautiful sights of the Workshop!

"Get Up and Do Your Job"

My father, Commander John H. Gannon, United States Navy Medical Service Corps, passed away suddenly on what would have been his and Mom's fifty-fourth wedding anniversary, August 6, 2014.

For the second time I prayed for the strength needed to be a joyous Santa during the Christmas season. This time it was extremely difficult. When Mom passed I had most of the year to come to terms with it...but Dad's passing was only three months before Santa season, truly horrid timing (if there is anything as "good" timing when losing a parent).

Fall began, and then Halloween (my other favorite time of year) and Thanksgiving neared. I simply was not in the right frame of mind to don the Red Suit that season. I was angry, hurt, devastated...and in severe denial.

Dad always looked forward to hearing each year's Santa stories, and I looked forward to telling him the tales to bring a smile to his face. But now he was gone, no longer present to hear the tales. My heart was ripped to shreds.

He is buried at the Beaufort National Cemetery, rejoined with my mother both on Earth and in Heaven. It was a lengthy visit to their resting place that returned me to where I needed to be. I prayed at their grave, asking...no, pleading...both God and my father for help and guidance for the future, immediate and long-term. I was in the most emotional turmoil of my life, and the steady logic that had always guided me forward was buried deep under storms of emotions.

It was a beautiful fall afternoon, bright blue skies and wisps of white clouds. I'll never forget a gentle breeze tickled the leaves of the trees in the cemetery, shuffling them about. I prayed long and silent; staring not at the headstone but at the ground above where they lay.

In my reverie, in that peaceful place, I heard my father so clearly say,

"Get up and do your job."

I did. In spite of my personal anguish, that year I gave, as always, every one of Santa's visitors the Christmas cheer they needed and deserved...and saved a little for myself as well...

A Fripp Face-lift

After sixteen Christmas seasons of receiving children and families in the middle of the courtyard of the Fripp Island Beach Club complex, Santa and Mama Claus were moved to a *new* set and backdrop in front of the Beach Club building. It was truly festive in appearance and a greater visible venue for the biggest crowd we'd ever had…it was joyously almost overwhelming!

It also marked the first time that Santa would take a photo with a turtle! Yes, little Franklin appeared a bit "shell-shocked" at taking a photo with ole' Saint Nick, and I'm still not sure if Franklin was smiling in his photo or not!

Another Perfect Moment Captured

There was another incredible out-take photo from the Captured Moments Photography studio shoots. Eric had finished the photo session with a little girl and as he was talking with her mother she was still in Santa's lap pointing at the book they had been holding as a prop. Eric saw the action continuing and started snapping that moment. The little lady's mom was so impressed with that photo she told both them and Santa they were free to use that photo for their own publicity! That photo became the cover photo of Santa's Facebook page for a year!

Photo courtesy Captured Moments Photography

www.cmoments.com

The Sleeping Santa & Baby

At one time a couple years ago there was a national craze of a photo of Santa who created a "sleeping pose" with a baby who was snoozing in his lap.

It was an incredible photo, and I give total applause to that Santa for creating that memorable scene.

I, like many other Santas, have been doing this type of pose for years but never thought about placing it online (or if my version has been posted by families I'm not aware of it). But, not to be outdone, I asked Eric of Captured Moments Photography to intentionally create our own *Sleeping Santa and Baby* photo as often as possible, whenever we had a baby who wanted nothing more than to sleep in Santa's arms, of course! Here's our version of Sleeping Santa and Baby…

Photo courtesy Captured Moments Photography

www.cmoments.com

"Toys For Tots" at Frampton Plantation

In December, 2014 Santa added yet another event to his Beaufort calendar, Toys for Tots at Frampton Plantation in Yemassee, South Carolina. It was a new event at this location, the home of the South Carolina Lowcountry Tourism Commission.

The mission of The U.S. Marine Corps Reserve Toys For Tots Program is to collect new, unwrapped toys during October, November and December each year, and distribute those toys as Christmas gifts to less fortunate children in the community in which the campaign is conducted. (http://toysfortots.org/)

I was invited to bring Santa to help raise toys for the Marine Corps to deliver to needy children. I immediately said "yes!" Local author Kim Poovey rejoined with Santa to read the Christmas story to the children gathered around the back of the house. It was an incredible way to end that Christmas season!

Kim and Frampton's Director of Visitors' Center Operations Lynn Bristow Cook even got to whisper their Christmas wishes to Santa at the same time!

Photos courtesy Kim Poovey

www.kimpoovey.com

Couldn't "Let Go" of This Christmas Party

A local Beaufort business had hired me to bring Santa to their events many times over the years. In 2014 they held it on our great Marine Corps Recruit Depot!

The event in particular was held on Parris Island at the Lyceum and *Frozen* the hit movie of 2013, was the theme. Santa got his photo with Anna and Elsa to take home and show Santa's family, in that *Frozen* was also the number one movie of the year at the North Pole Workshop Complex!

When asked why he agreed to do this themed party, Santa simply said, "I couldn't let it go."

Yes, boys and girls, Santa does really bad puns with songs Mommy and Daddy are tired of hearing…

cr ic
ME2
Barby
Maycap

and a Modall-
clayu Mare-
cers

2 pq
10E
PolyPo Kit
sl

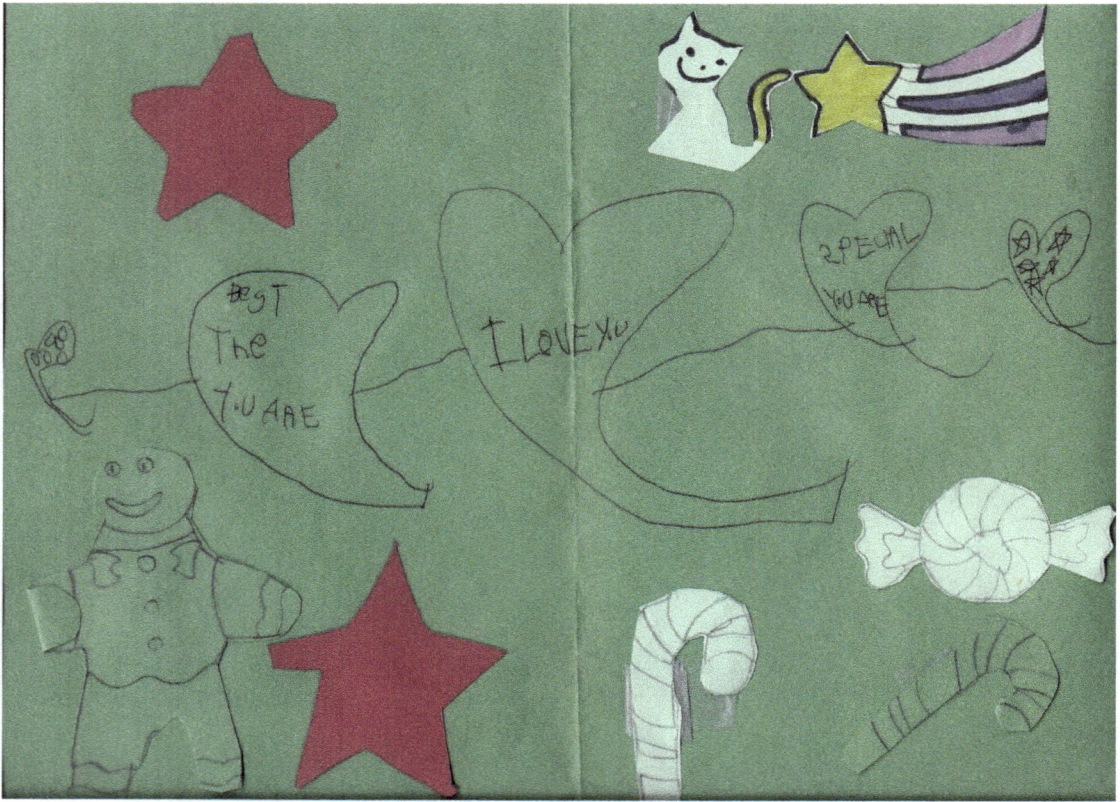

Santa loves all the drawings made by children- 2005

Dear Santa,
Please bring me a Nintendo DS, and some games. Also, I want a jet pack.
Thank you,

Holden
Hollo

P.S. I was really good.

Holden was really reaching for the sky with his Christmas wish in 2007!

Part 5

The Closing Claus

The Conversation... and Decision

In early fall of 2015, I sat down with my wife and had *The Conversation* I always knew would come one day, but didn't expect so soon. The 2015 Beaufort Christmas Season would have to be my last as Beaufort's Santa Claus.

My personal health and physical abilities had been recently declining due to various medical problems. It was becoming noticeable to the crowds at events. Santa's great weight-loss from 300 to 235 pounds in a year, for example, was prompting questions like "Looking kinda skinny, Santa?" Santa would usually reply, "Mama Claus says no chocolate chip cookies until Christmas Eve" and so forth. Santa was walking with a now-prominent limp, and relied more obviously on that candy-cane colored walking cane. Thankfully, Main Street Beaufort was kind enough to provide a golf cart to move Santa from the Old Bay Marketplace to the tree lighting from 2013-2015. Working the large events at Cat Island, Fripp Island, and Chick-Fil-A, however, was taking their toll on me. Walking and shoulder movements had become excruciating and exhausting. Even holding objects of any weight were nearly impossible. Ironically, the scheduled events in 2015 for Santa were at nearly an all-time record.

I remained diligent to the end of the year. However, the time had definitely come to hang up the Red Suit and put the Black Boots on their closet shelf. Notifying all the businesses and companies was predictably difficult for me on a personal level, but I decided not to tell anyone until after the 2015 Santa Season had concluded.

Mrs. Claus was, as always, on hand to help Santa at Fripp Island, along with Fripp Elf JT. It was a beautiful weekend, the Friday and Saturday after Thanksgiving, and the weather was God-graced perfection. Additionally, Santa was granted a once-in-a-lifetime extraordinary memory to make 2015 the most special!

Santa and Mrs. Claus were set up back in the courtyard in his gold and red-velvet high-backed chair. A Deejay had been hired for the first time ever. (Several years ago, if I may interject, Santa and Mama were taking a break between visitors on Saturday morning's *Breakfast with The Clauses* when a young man asked if his girlfriend could sit in Santa's chair after their visit with them, to which Santa said "of course". We milled about, stretching our legs for a few minutes. All watched as the young man got down on one knee and proposed to his lady love in Santa's chair!) I say that to lead into a very similar event and our finest Fripp Island moment ever. A young lady and her boyfriend were next in line and someone quickly whispered into Santa's ear to not let the young lady off his knee after the photos were taken. Sitting on his knee she whispered, "I am so embarrassed to be sitting here!" Santa, naturally, reassured her, "No one's ever supposed to be embarrassed. This is Christmastime! A time to celebrate!" The young lady began to stand, but Santa held a firm grip around her waist to keep her in place. Seconds later, her boyfriend got down on one knee to propose. That was the secret whispered in Santa's ear, and that was the only time in twenty-three years that Santa Claus was part of a marriage proposal!

Proposal on Santa's knee

Screen Capture Source: Instagram frippislandrsrt

I called Kelly (Poinsettia) before Thanksgiving and told her about my retirement plan, but I wanted to keep it a secret from everyone until after my Santa season was complete. I was going to need a lot of help with my arms as I was no longer able to lift children as I once could.

Poinsettia came back after the Fripp Island weekend for one more season, helping to lift the children onto Santa's lap. (I hoped that no one would see the physical pain that I endured under Santa's visage.)

The Beaufort Christmas Parade grew exponentially in twenty-three seasons. Beaufort Fire Department's Tower 1 fire truck had already been retired, so I was riding in the bucket of the Tower 2 truck in 2015. The parade was so long and large that there was barely enough street space to hold every vehicle in the parade. By the time the parade was over, the color guard leading the front of the parade rapidly converged on our bumper, making it seem as if it were a never-ending parade for a couple minutes!

Again we were blessed with a heavenly day of blue skies and perfect temperature to celebrate my last Parade in The Red Suit.

Photos courtesy Captured Moments Photography

www.cmoments.com

Photos courtesy Captured Moments Photography

www.cmoments.com

Santa with LaNelle Fabian, Main Street Beaufort Director

Christmas Magic!

In the era of today's modern technology there were still another few firsts in Santa's long career in Beaufort.

It was another great day of studio photos at Captured Moments Photography, and we were doing something new for our customers that day. Eric and Susan wanted to increase the magic of this year's Santa photos by adding some special effects to the photos. Lighting effects were set up to make it appear as Christmas twinkles were coming from his bag of presents or the Christmas book Santa was reading with children. The results were truly magical...and gorgeous.

One of the rarest of moments for Santa was when twin newborns were brought in for their first Christmas photo!

Photos courtesy Captured Moments Photography

www.cmoments.com

A Royal Arrival

Santa traveled to the Royal Pines Country Club to bring Christmas cheer to the Royal Pines subdivision's families' gathering. Kelly even brought her sons on to join Santa and Poinsettia as Junior Elves, giving it a truly memorable time for those boys as well as the visiting families! It was easy to see that the Santa Family had a dog-gone good time!

Photos courtesy Sue Jarrett

www.suejarrett.com

Santa even got into the festive spirit and joined in a sing-along of *Santa Claus Is Comin' To Town!* He didn't even need any eggnog to help that deep voice stay in perfect key!

A Chick-Fil-A Reunion

Photo courtesy Sue Jarrett

www.suejarrett.com

Sue Jarrett was also the photographer for the 2015 Chick-Fil-A shoot.

Sue published book of wildlife photos (*Daddy, Mommy and Me*) from her trek to South Africa, and Santa was more than happy to take a photo while reading her book! (Yes, you need to get a copy, the images are breathtaking!)

Her First Photo After 20 Years of Photos

I can never say enough just how much Santa Claus appreciated all the help his elves gave him over the years, especially Poinsettia's invaluable help during the 2015 Christmas Season. She helped hide my growing weakness in legs and arms as we posed with many hundreds of happy and excited children and pets all month. Before we wrapped up the season completely we did a photo that had never been done…Santa with Kelly herself, in civilian clothes for the only time in two decades! And Santa even brought some snow to make it the most special photo ever!

"Tot's All, Folks..."

Finally, the last Santa event arrived. It was the second annual Toys for Tots event at Frampton Plantation (Lowcountry Tourism Commission), in Yemassee, SC.

The Frampton staff invited the Marine Corps from nearby Beaufort, Santa, Cappy the Clown from Hilton Head Island, the Charles Towne Few Pirates from Charleston, and Sons of the Confederate Veterans (Camp 2100 from Ridgeland), authors, and more! One of the pirates was dressed in his Santa-mimicking finest, and he and Saint Nick were definitely festive for the event! Three large boxes of toys were collected for needy and deserving children.

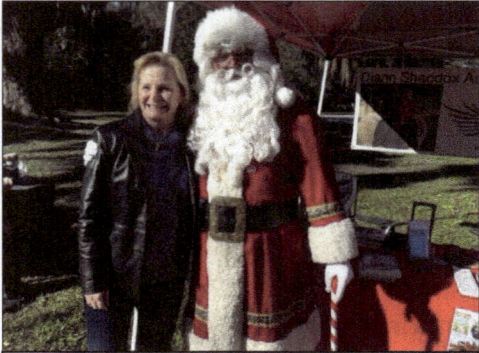
Santa & author Diann Shaddox
www.diannshaddox.com

Santa & Cappy The Clown
www.clounaround.com

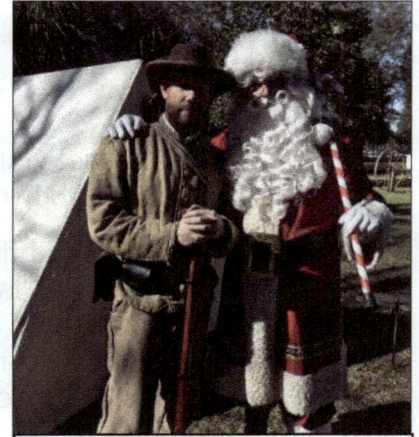
Santa & Michael Skinner
SOCV Camp 2100

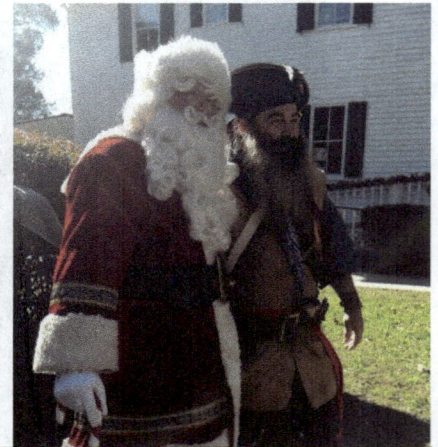
Santa with The Charles Towne Few Pirates

(can be found on Facebook)

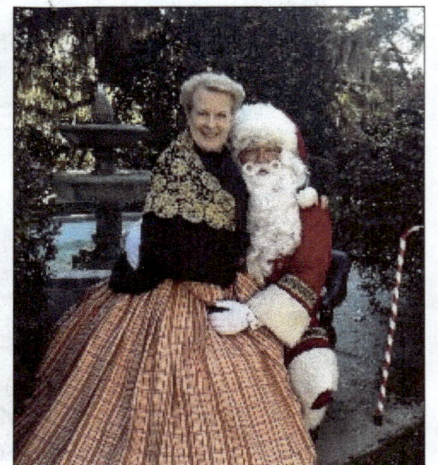
Santa with the Frampton Plantation Staff: Peach Morrison, Allyson Jones, Lynn Bristow Cook

www.southcarolinalowcountry.com

The Reality of...the Reality...

Santa with Beaufort Fire Department's Captain John
Robinson, his mother Frances, and his son after the
2015 Beaufort Christmas Parade

On December 19, 2015, I gathered my Santa suits and accessories (beards, mustaches, gloves, boots, and the like) and, with a bit of melancholy, I hung them in the closet for the last time, next to Mrs. Claus' dresses (which were already retired after the last Fripp Island weekend). I stared at the red velvet cloth, stroked the softness of the outfits, focusing on the gold brocade trim and its painstaking perfect stitching. There were minutes of sadness, knowing there would be no more rides in fire trucks, waving to the crowds in the annual Christmas Parade, leading the tree lighting in downtown Beaufort, or the beach club lighting on Fripp Island. Was this sorrow for me, or for the multitudes of people who flocked to Beaufort Christmas events with the Santa they had known for over two decades? I think perhaps it was a combination of both.

At the same time, it was joyous. Having the strength of mind and soul, I knew that God had answered my prayers throughout the last couple of years. He gave me the tenacity to gracefully get through what turned out to be the second-busiest Santa season in my career. Physical pain and illness had taken over my body far too early, but the personal discomfort was tempered by the memories of hundreds of families across upper Beaufort County who had another joyous Christmas celebration during the Beaufort Christmas season, and another year of wonderful fun visits with Saint Nick.

In February of 2016 I decided that simply retiring wasn't the proper thing to do. I never intended twenty-three years ago to become THE Santa for all the major events in the upper county, never mind to be the Santa at so many local companies' Christmas parties. At any time, any one of the companies could have chosen someone else to don the Red Suit at their Christmas events, but they always called me. In more recent years it required a lot of schedule juggling to fit everyone into the three weeks I would appear after Thanksgiving, but every year it all worked out. The various businesses saw me only at their locations, but rarely saw me as Santa elsewhere in our community. A book had to be written, I felt, and it had to be a "Thank You" to everyone.

Browsing through the thousands of Santa photo files on my computer helped to recall a multitude of appearances which started so long ago, way back in 1993. I even discovered some old articles from *The Beaufort Gazette*, black and white newspapers now yellowed by age, of my Santa in his earliest days. Clicking through the thousands of photos brought a smile to my face, and a good Santa chuckle while viewing the photos of me with dogs, cats, children, teenagers, adults, full families, snakes, birds, and even Franklin the Turtle!

Twenty-three years. Still, as I write these words, it doesn't feel like twenty-three years. It seems like only yesterday when I first walked out of the Old Bay Marketplace and onto Bay Street in that very first Santa suit…and all the babies with whom I was honored to take "First Christmas Pictures", and how many, as grown-ups, brought their own the last couple years…

I know that my Santa and Santa Family members are in photo albums, on mantles, and walls all across the globe. I am honored that we are part of so many families' Christmas memories.

Maintain the Reality of the Illusion was the mantra I'd set for myself and the entire Santa Family for its career: never break character, and assuring all children had a visit with Santa for as long as they wanted. My sole purpose and dream, once I realized this was going to be a long-term venture, was to make sure all visitors left with a positive, joyous visit, and a memory which gave them all hopes and dreams of their own. I can honestly and proudly say that I, with Mama Claus and all The Elves, did that job to the absolute best of our abilities.

Santa at the Preserve at Port Royal 2015

Christmas thanks go to so many people for allowing me, and helping me, to bring Santa to their events over the past twenty-three years:

- LaNelle Fabian, my final Director of Main Street Beaufort

- The Beaufort, South Carolina, Fire Department for its safe transport of Santa Claus and his family through twenty-two Christmas Parades

- Jeannine Taylor, the elf "JT" for two decades at Fripp Island Resort, and Collins Strickland, Recreation Director at Fripp Island Resort

- Peggy Hopkins of Sanctuary Golf Club on Cat Island

- Fran Pund Tuttle of Lowcountry Produce Market and Cafe in Beaufort

- Seth and Cynthia Scarpa of Chick-Fil-A in Beaufort

- Aleisia Ashlaw of the Beaufort Academy of Dance

- Rose Ewing of Helena Place in Port Royal

- Eric and Susan Smith of Captured Moments Photography in Beaufort

- Sue Jarrett for her help as Santa's photographer from the first days to the last

- Todd Stowe for the fun photo years at Chick-Fil-A in Beaufort

- All the companies and communities who invited Santa Claus and the Santa Family members to their own special Christmas events over the decades

- Mayors David Taub and Billy Keyserling for the years they lit the city Christmas tree with Santa Claus at Night On The Town

- Dennis Adams for helping craft the tradition of Santa joining him on stage during the reading of The Christmas Story

- Julie O'Connell Evans, Kelly O'Connell Lesesne, and Samantha Caron Franklin, for donning the red and green tunics as Santa's elves

- And most especially, my greatest thanks to my wife Mendy, for the courage to put on those heavy red dresses and introduce Mrs. Claus to three generations of children and their families, and for parting with me for many December weekends and nights so that Santa could visit so many wonderful children and families.

Finally, to the thousands of families across the world who visited Santa and Mama and The Elves for twenty-three joyous Christmas seasons: you will always be in my heart and soul this Christmas, and every Christmas to come. Thank you for the memoires, and may God Bless You All...

"Happy Christmas to all...

…and to all a Good Night!"

Photo courtesy Captured Moments Photography

www.cmoments.com

THE AUTHOR

Jack Gannon is the son of the late Commander John H. Gannon, United States Navy Medical Service Corps, and the late Margaret O. Gannon, both of whom are interred at Beaufort National Cemetery, only 3 miles from where Jack lives. His parents raised him on or near multiple naval bases across the country, from coast to coast and as far west as Kaneohe, Hawaii, from where he has his earliest memories.

As a child, his favorite fictional character was Clark Kent of the Daily Planet, not his other identity of Superman! He was fascinated with the news staff in the comics, getting information of things happening before they made it into the newspaper, and that began a very early interest in print media and writing. While attending Fork Union Military Academy in Virginia he worked on the lower school newspaper *The Bayonet* and the academy yearbook, including one year when he wrote the dedication for the lower school's section of the book.

His studies at Winthrop College (now University) in Rock Hill, SC, focused in communications with an emphasis on newspaper and television news. However, his career goal was tossed aside when his mother suffered a massive stroke a week before he received his Bachelor of Arts degree. He elected to leave his media career plans behind and return home to help his father care for his mother, and worked a couple of local jobs before gaining a position in The Beaufort Gazette's circulation department as its mailroom supervisor in 1987. During the next fourteen years he worked his way to a front office position until the Gazette and its sister paper, The Island Packet, began merging operations. He was then transferred to the Packet's offices in Bluffton, SC, to manage the customer service staff handling subscribers' delivery needs for both papers.

His newspaper career ended in 2011 and he started planning how to fill his days, when he was reunited with his Beaufort High School best friend Cyndi Williams-Barnier. During their school years, they talked about writing books together after they graduated college, but lost contact with each other after high school graduation.

Thirty-two years later, after their first dinner together with their spouses, they got around to asking each other, "Where's that book you were going to write?" Both now retired, they immediately picked up where they left off and began writing those decades-old stories, and formed their own writing partnership, J&C Wordsmiths, LLC. Their stories are action/adventure/suspense and fantasy/paranormal, with this book adding the historical/autobiographical genre.

Jack decided to medically-retire from his Lowcountry Santa position after twenty-three years, but felt that simply retiring after all that time wasn't very polite. He needed to say "thank you" to everyone who kept asking him to bring his Santa and North Pole Family to their events year after year, and the result is the memoir in your hands, "I WALKED IN SANTA'S BOOTS".

When not writing, Jack prefers the tranquility of his Beaufort, South Carolina home with his wife, Mendy, and Pomeranian, Tasia.

CONTACT INFORMATION

Please follow the author on his websites and Facebook author page:

www.gannons.com

www.jandcwordsmiths.com

www.facebook.com/jandcwordsmiths

More photos of Santa Claus across the decades can be found at this book's Facebook page:

www.facebook.com/santaclausbeaufortsc

"And remember to be good, for goodness' sake!"

Photo courtesy Captured Moments Photography

www.cmoments.com

www.ingramcontent.com/pod-product-compliance
Lightning Source LLC
Chambersburg PA
CBHW061959090426
42811CB00006B/983